# HOMELANDS OF THE SCOTS

A guide to territories
and locations of historic interest
connected with the Clans and Major Families
of Scotland.

## Roderick Martine

Published by Spurbooks
in association with the
British Tourist Authority and the
International Gathering Trust.
Line drawings and cover photograph by courtesy
of the Scottish Tourist Board.

Published by
SPURBOOKS
(a division of Holmes McDougall Ltd)
Allander House
137-141 Leith Walk
Edinburgh EH6 8NS

ISBN 0 7157 2075 9

© Spurbooks, 1981

Printed in Great Britain
by Holmes McDougall Limited, Edinburgh

'Clan family is beyond and outside and above divisions between nations, countries and continents . . . it takes no note of age and sex, rank or wealth, success or failure. The spiritual link of clanship embraces them all.'

*Dame Flora MacLeod of MacLeod*
1878–1977

The author wishes to acknowledge the co-operation of the following:

His Grace the Duke of Argyll
The Rt Hon Earl of Cromarty
The Rt Hon Earl of Elgin & Kincardine
Sir Crispin Agnew of Lochnaw
Mrs Guthrie of Guthrie
Mr Alastair Campbell, Yr of Airds
Clan Hannay Society
Clan Chattan Association
The Stewart Society
Norman H. MacDonald, FSA Scot
E. H. Armstrong, FSA Scot
Douglas G. Gair, CLJ, FRSPB
John Turnbull Esq,

and the many others who assisted in compiling this information.

# Contents

|     | MacCallum (See Malcolm) |
|-----|-------------------------|
|     | MacCallum (See Malcolm) |
| 120 | MacColl |
| 121 | MacCorquodale |
| 122 | MacCulloch |
| 123 | MacDonald |
| 127 | MacDougall |
| 128 | MacDuff |
|     | MacDuffie (See MacFie) |
| 129 | MacEwen |
| 130 | MacFarlane |
| 131 | MacFie (MacPhee) |
| 132 | MacGillivray (See also Chattan) |
| 133 | MacGregor |
| 134 | MacInnes |
| 135 | MacIntyre (See also Chattan) |
| 136 | MacIver |
| 137 | Mackay |
| 138 | Mackenzie |
| 140 | Mackinlay |
| 141 | Mackinnon |
| 142 | Mackintosh (See also Chattan) |
| 143 | MacLachlan |
| 144 | MacLaine of Lochbuie (See also Maclean) |
| 145 | Maclaren (Clan Labhran) |
|     | MacLennan (See Logan) |
| 146 | Maclean (See also MacLaine of Lochbuie) |
| 147 | MacLeod |
|     | MacGowan (See Gow) |
|     | MacKendrick (See Henderson) |
| 149 | Macmillan |
| 150 | MacNab |
| 151 | MacNaughton |
| 152 | MacNeil |
| 153 | MacPhail (See also Chattan) |
| 154 | Macpherson (See also Chattan) |
| 155 | Macquarrie |
| 156 | MacQueen (See also Chattan) |
| 157 | Macrae |
| 158 | MacThomas (See also Chattan) |
| 159 | Maitland |
| 160 | Malcolm |
| 161 | Marjoriebanks |
| 162 | Matheson (Mathieson) |
| 163 | Maxwell |
| 165 | Menzies |

# Foreword

The main reason to prompt a commendation of this book is that land and people have for so long gone together in Scotland. Only the impact of the Industrial Revolution weakened this tie.

While it is true that the Sovereign, in earliest times, made large grants of land to be held as Earldoms by the great magnates, whose lesser grants were often of considerable size, it was not until the reign of King Robert I that the King, in redistributing responsibility, began to favour quite small landowners — at £10 value a year. Thus it was increasingly the case that relatively small areas of land became identified with the same name over many generations; and so small were they that, as each generation succeeded, the younger sons perforce had to make their way in the world. Many of them emigrated altogether, and yet, over the years, will quite correctly look to the land as their source of origin, even although it is in a different ownership, occupancy or use.

The same is true of tenant occupancy. There must be great numbers of people whose forebears were tenant farmers, resident on farms perhaps for several generations; and it is of abiding interest to the descendants to track down these farms and see the nature of the country in which their forebears worked.

In the Highlands the clan system produced a somewhat different story as the years unfolded. Here the Chiefs exerted their rights of ownership in most of the original cases by force of arms and "use and wont". The pattern of family, name and land was of a more paternal, rather than a feudal, nature. However, in general terms it is often possible to identify a part of Scotland within a Clan area as being the most likely place descendants should visit to search for still tangible evidence.

There are other imponderables also, where you have an heiress marrying another landowner, and her name and land become merged and buried in his.

In all researches you will require utmost diligence and accuracy, and a book such as this will, I believe, be a great help to bring what might only be considered as landscape into a fascinating story of real people, their lives, hopes and ambitions, successes and failures.

*The Rt. Hon. The Earl of Elgin and Kincardine, DL, JP.*

# Introduction

Scotland spreads over 30,411 square miles of land — land as diverse as the rich farmland of the southern Borders and the lush coastal plains of the east, the harsh, spectacular scenery of the Highlands and, offshore, the scattered islands of the West. Scotland occupies the northern 37 per cent of the main British Isles, and itself encompasses several races. The Romans gave the name of Caledonia to present-day Scotland and called the inhabitants Caledonians. The original Scots, however, a Celtic, Gaelic-speaking race, came from Ireland. For years they vied for superiority with the established Pictish tribes while Norsemen colonised the far north, spreading into the central Highlands. Kenneth I (Mac Alpin) was the first Scot to rule both Picts and Scots in 843AD, but in the 11th and 12th centuries, the Normans of William the Conqueror made their way up from England to settle and integrate.

It was a 14th-century Norman knight, Robert Bruce, Earl of Carrick, who first truly united the diverse factions into a recognised and governable kingdom. The death of Alexander III and subsequent death of his daughter and heir, Margaret of Norway, had brought a period of puppet government under John Baliol. Through Bruce's descent from William the Lion, he was able to make a claim to the Scottish throne in defiance of Edward I of England, who saw himself as over-lord. Bruce's subsequent victory over Edward II at Bannockburn in 1314 laid the foundation for the national identity upon which his turbulent Stewart descendants were to build.

But more than in any other part of the British Isles, it was the great Lowland families and particularly the mighty Highland clans with their unique feudal and egalitarian societies who came to characterise the territories in which they lived. In the Highlands, each area of clan country became something of a realm within itself. Loyalties lay not foremost to the anointed sovereign, but to a chief, who could allocate such loyalty according to his own judgement. That government in Stirling, Fife or Edinburgh should appear remote to the Highlander might not seem surprising — imagine how many must have felt after James VI and I had taken his court south to London.

The word 'clan' is Gaelic for 'children', and the meaning implies members of a family. In various parts of the Highlands, at differing periods of history, groups of people, usually related, either native to the area, or settled through circumstance or grant of lands, banded together, usually for protection against their neighbours. In doing so, a recognised identity was created, and these 'clans' would pay allegiance to a recognised leader, their chief, whose position was usually hereditary. Times were rough, and when a chief did not turn out to be what was required, he might be supplanted by a stronger close relative. Although the powers of a chief were all-embracing, there was a code of conduct between clansfolk which made every man his master's equal. Loyalty was unquestioned.

Often members of a clan would only hold christian names, derived from parentage; Lachlan, son of Lachlan or 'Mac' Lachlan. The vernacular inevitably created varied spellings and pronunciation, and nicknames were given for further identification or names were related to specific activities within the clan: the MacSporrans were hereditary pursebearers to the Lords of the Isles; Fletcher, which means 'arrow maker' from the word 'flêchier', is a sept name of Clan Gregor. Families bearing a name that was different from the main name of a clan, but who were associated with, or dependent on, a clan, were called 'septs'. Situations arose where one clan incorporated innumerable different names. When the MacGregors were outlawed in the seventeenth century, and not allowed to bear their own name, many clansmen took such names as Black or White.

It is important to differentiate, however, between the clans as such, and the Border families, usually of Norman origin, who maintained a basic feudal system. Although a Border Earl could invariably field an army of men in battle, these were mostly tenants or vassals from his lands, and he rarely commanded the unquestioned devotion given to his Highland counterpart.

Throughout their dynasty, the Stewart kings were kept fully occupied with controlling their unruly and independent-minded subjects. Certain families, such as the House of Douglas, rose to such prominence and wealth that they had to be checked. The Clan Donald at one time controlled the whole of the western seaboard as far south as the Isle of Man. In controlling the north, it was necessary to appoint Lord High Justiciars such as Robert II's son, known as the Wolf of Badenoch, whose brutal but effective measures and complete dominance of the region brought problems of their own.

When James VI's court moved to London, the

Highlanders, in particular, maintained a fierce independence. It was this that Cromwell's supporters encountered in their battles with the Royalist Montrose; and it was this that eventually led to the contrived destruction of the clan system. When James VII and II was deposed by his daughter in 1688, nobody could foresee the long-term impact it would have on his northern kingdom.

In theory, George I of the House of Hanover, being a great-grandson of James VI, and most importantly, Protestant, should have been quite acceptable, although he spoke little English. There were those, however, who had not felt strongly about James VII's conversion to Catholicism, and who saw his heirs, by his second wife, as the rightful claimants to the British throne. The Highland Scots in particular were unsympathetic towards Hanoverian rule. The Stuarts, the 'Kings across the Water', James VII's son and grandsons, were to bring great suffering to Scotland with the uprisings they incited in 1715 and 1745, but at the same time they brought great dignity, colour, hope and romance, culminating in their final crushing defeat at the Battle of Culloden in 1746, an event which was irrevocably to obliterate a way of life.

From this point, following the reprisals conducted by the Duke of Cumberland's soldiers, the Whig parliament took measures to ensure once and for all that the Highland clans would never again rise in defiance of the government of the land. The Acts of Proscription of 1747 made the wearing of tartan, seen as a uniform of rebellion, illegal; a policy of depopulating land in favour of sheep-farming was imposed, leading to massive clearances of the crofting community, the clansfolk on whose support a chief relied.

Contrary to popular impression, few of the Highland chiefs were directly involved with the clearing process. Although the few that were owned large areas of land, many chiefs were forced into personal economic hardship through their attempts to protect dependants. Although the Clearances can be seen as one of the most cruel and shameful events in a long and violent history, there is evidence to suggest that in the following years, had they not taken place, a worse evil in the shape of famine would have affected Scotland as it did Ireland.

As it was, thousands were dispossessed of their homes and forced to emigrate to Canada, America, New Zealand and Australia. There, against hostile conditions, many prospered, bringing all the inherent finer qualities of their race to bear upon the communities in which they settled. The Scots have gained a world reputation for thrift, honesty and an ability to work hard. In the New World, every man could become a 'bonnet laird'. The continuance and popularity of clan, family, Caledonian and St Andrew Societies around the world bears testimony to the spread and influence of the ex-patriate Scot. Further, it proves that the concept of kinship relating to the lands of our forefathers is as strong as ever.

Sir Walter Scott, King George IV and Queen Victoria created fashions for the 'romance' of the Highlands in the nineteenth century. Tartans were revived under their influence, and many lowland families who would hitherto have shuddered at a connection with what they considered heathen, Highland clans and what they stood for, rushed to involve themselves in the glamour of what some call 'tartan-mania'. Border families had tartans designed and patented to their names and the kilt became recognised as Scotland's national dress.

Many who come to Scotland are confused by the mass of literature available. The purpose of this book is to direct readers to the areas and places of interest directly associated with clan or family, to indicate whether a name is 'Highland' or 'Lowland', and to outline briefly the histories associated with a name.

This book is far from comprehensive and is designed simply to put readers on the right track. For further information, Clan Societies, Family Associations and historic records should be consulted. For sources of information not included under clan/family sections, there is a general list of information centres and locations of interest.

NB: Where possible, the author has stated whether or not properties or sites are accessible to the general public. A number of locations, however, are privately owned and, understandably, property holders do not welcome invasion of privacy. It is suggested that local enquiries and/or advance contact with house- or land-owner or agent should be instigated before a visit is made. This is a matter of courtesy and should prevent disappointment.

# Places of General Interest

## Famous Battlefields

### CENTRAL

STIRLING
*Bannockburn,* South of Stirling off M80.
The battle on 23–24 June 1314 at which Robert Bruce routed the English army of Edward II and firmly established himself as King of Scots.
Bannockburn Memorial and Visitor Centre. Site under care of National Trust for Scotland. Open April–Sept.

### HIGHLAND

INVERNESS
*Culloden Moor,* East of Inverness on B9006.
The battle took place on 16 April 1746 between the army of Prince Charles Edward Stuart and the Duke of Cumberland's forces representing the Hanoverian government. The Young Pretender's defeat ended all hopes that the Stuarts might regain the British throne.
A tall cairn (1881) commemorates the fallen. Scattered stones marked with the names of Clans show the graves of the Highlanders. The Cumberland stone marks the position taken by Cumberland before the battle.
National Trust for Scotland Visitor Centre and Leanach Battle Museum. Open April–mid Oct. Battlefield area accessible all the year round.

### LOTHIAN

EAST LOTHIAN
*Prestonpans,* A198.
Cairn commemorates battle fought against Cope's Government forces by Prince Charles Edward Stuart, in 1745: the Prince's first great victory.

### STRATHCLYDE

CUNNING-
HAME
*Largs.* Here in 1263, Alexander III fought Hakon, King of Norway, on both sea and land. The Scots won after two days, resulting in their acquiring the Hebrides and the Isle of Man, which had been held by the Norwegians for 400 years.

## TAYSIDE

ANGUS      Arbroath Abbey Church, Arbroath. On 6 April 1320, a letter to Pope John XXII acknowledging Robert Bruce as rightful King of Scots was sent from here by the Estates of Scotland.

PERTH & KINROSS      *Killiecrankie,* on A9.
Battle fought 27 July 1689 against government by Graham of Claverhouse, Viscount Dundee, and his Jacobite followers. Although the Jacobites won the battle, Dundee was fatally wounded and three weeks later the Highlanders were decisively defeated at Dunkeld.
National Trust for Scotland Visitor Centre. Open April-Oct.

# Famous Castles

## CENTRAL

STIRLING      *Stirling Castle,* centre of town. Most of building seen today dates from the fifteenth and sixteenth centuries. Attractions include Landmark Visitor Centre on Esplanade. Open all the year round.

## LOTHIAN

EDINBURGH CITY      *Edinburgh Castle,* centre of city. Fortress from earliest times. Malcolm Canmore lived here in the eleventh century. Queen Margaret's Chapel dates from 1076. The Esplanade is always open. Among the attractions: Scottish Regalia and Mons Meg. One o'clock gun. Open all the year round.

Mons Meg

*Holyrood Palace.* The name means Holy Cross, and is believed to have come from the fragment of the cross of Jesus held by Queen Margaret, wife of Malcolm Canmore. Her son, King David I founded the Abbey, which stands behind the palace. Holyrood is the official residence of Her Majesty the Queen when she visits Edinburgh. The Palace was begun in the sixteenth century by James IV. Mary, Queen of Scots came here from France in 1561, and it was in her apartments here that Rizzio was murdered. Since James VI's departure to London, the palace has never been occupied for any length of time by a reigning monarch. Open all year. Closed for State Visits.

## WEST LOTHIAN

LINLITHGOW     *Linlithgow Palace.* Oldest part built by Edward I in 1302. Mary, Queen of Scots was born here in 1542, as had been her father in 1512. Charles I was the last monarch to sleep in the Palace, and in 1914 King George V held a court here. Open all year.

# Agnew

The Agnews of Lochnaw became Hereditary Sheriffs of Wigton in 1451. The first of the name in Scotland is William des Aigneu, who, in Liddesdale around 1190, witnessed a charter between Ranulf de Soulis and Jedburgh Abbey. Andrew Agnew, however, was first of family on record when he was appointed Constable of Lochnaw Castle in 1426.

A branch of the family went to Ulster and obtained a grant of lands near Larne from James VI. Their castle, Kilwaughter, is now a ruin, but many families from the USA and Australia descend from this line.

**PLACES of INTEREST**

**DUMFRIES AND GALLOWAY**

WIGTOWN

*Castle Wig,* Drumastoun, near Whithorn. Lands and Barony acquired by Andrew, 5th Sheriff, 1543. *Dalreagle,* a farm, was another residence here. *Innermessan Castle.* Ruin. Seat of Chiefs until purchased by Earl of Stair, 1723.
*Lochnaw Castle,* Stranraer. Thirteenth century castle. Ruin on island in loch. Later *Lochnaw Castle* (fifteenth century keep) on shores of loch, run as a guest house.
*Lochryan House,* Cairnryan. Built by Col. James Agnew. Occupied by Wallace family who acquired it through marriage. No admission.
*Old Leswalt Kirkyard* — Agnew Mausoleum. 6th Sheriff buried with Protestant rites 1590. Memorial Tower to Sir Andrew, 7th Baronet.

**LOTHIAN**

EDINBURGH CITY

*Edinburgh Castle.* Sir Patrick, 8th Sheriff created Baronet of Nova Scotia and invested here. Plaque recalls the event.
*Scottish National Portrait Gallery.* Portrait of Sir Andrew Agnew of

Lochnaw, 5th Baronet.
*National Gallery of Scotland.* Portrait of
Lady Agnew of Lochnaw by Sargeant.

# Anderson or MacAndrew

This surname is strongly connected with St Andrew, the patron saint of Scotland, although it is common in both Aberdeenshire and the Lowlands. The Andersons or MacAndrews are probably connected with the Clan Anrias, a sept of Clan Ross. These MacAndrews are regarded as being connected with the Clan Chattan federation, and settled in Connage of Petty. Prominent branches of Clan Anderson are the Andersons of Dowhill, of West Ardbreck in Banffshire, and of Candacraig in Strathdon. Arms were awarded in the sixteenth century to Anderson of that Ilk, but his family has not yet been identified. The Chiefship has remained dormant for centuries. There are no locations specifically identified with this name.

| **PLACES of INTEREST** | **HIGHLAND** | |
|---|---|---|
| | INVERNESS | *Petty* is situated 1½ miles SW of Dalcross and 5 miles NE of Inverness. It is located on the Moray Firth. |

# Angus

This name means 'Unique Choice'. An Angus was king of Dalriada in the ninth century. The name is associated with Clan MacInnes, who are believed to have evolved from the Dalriads.

The Earldom of Angus was held by the Stewarts and Douglases and is now vested in the Dukedom of Hamilton.

| | | |
|---|---|---|
| **PLACES of INTEREST** | **LOTHIAN** | |
| | EAST LOTHIAN | *Athelstaneford,* N.E. of Haddington, B1343. Angus (d. 761), son of Fergus, King of Picts, led campaigns against the Scots, Britons and Angles. Legend has it that at Athelstaneford, he won a victory through the intervention of St Andrew, seeing a white cross in the sky. |
| | **TAYSIDE** | |
| | ANGUS | District of *Angus* formerly Forfarshire, an area of 873.5 sq m on East coast, north of Firth of Tay. |
| | PERTH AND KINROSS | *Abernethy,* A913. A seat of Pictish kings. Lands owned by Earls of Angus of various families. |

# Arbuthnot

The surname adopted by Duncan, son and heir to Hugh of Swinton from Berwickshire. The latter had received the lands of Arbuthnott in Kincardineshire from Walter Olifard at the end of the twelfth century. The family still hold the lands.

**PLACES of INTEREST**

**GRAMPIAN**

KINCARDINE AND DEESIDE

*Arbuthnott,* B967. Lands granted to Walter Olifard by William the Lion around 1175, almost certainly as a knight's fee.

*Arbuthnott Church.* Dedicated to St Ternay, dates from thirteenth century.

*Arbuthnott House,* 8 miles SW of Stonehaven. Sixteenth–eighteenth century. Superseded a thirteenth-century tower. (Open by arrangement, telephone Inverbervie 226.)

*Arbuthnott Aisle.* Burial place of the family.

# Armstrong

Alexander, first chief, held the ancient seat of Mangerton in Liddesdale, Roxburghshire, in the late thirteenth century. Originally Northmen, the Armstrongs came via Normandy or Northumbria, becoming expert light horsemen. They could field 3000 at their zenith. They held lands in Ewesdale, Eskdale and Annandale.

In 1363, Gilbert Armstrong was Scotland's ambassador to England. In 1610, the clan was 'broken' on the death of the 10th chief, but for many its pride was restored on the night of the Moon Landing on 21st July 1969. Neil Armstrong, the first man to walk on the moon, surely has some good Border blood in his ancestry. A fragment of Armstrong tartan taken by him on his journey now resides permanently at the Museum of Scottish Tartans in Comrie, Perthshire. The first gathering for nearly 400 years was held at the Tourneyholm in Liddesdale in 1979.

---

**PLACES of INTEREST**

**BORDERS**

ROXBURGH

*Caerlanrig Kirkyard*, Teviothead, 8½ miles S of Hawick. Memorial to Johnnie Armstrong and his followers.
*Ettleton Kirkyard*, Mangerton, 1 mile S of Newcastleton. On hill above Millholm Cross; ancient burial place of the clan.
*Hermitage Castle*. Just off Hawick-Newcastleton road, B6399. Clan's second chief murdered here — after saving his host's life. Open to public.
*Holehouse (Hollows Tower)* or *Gilnockie Tower,* Canonbie: on A7, 12 miles from Newcastleton. 1588 stronghold of Johnnie Armstrong of Gilnockie, hanged by King James V. Open 10am-5pm except Monday.

---

# Baird

The name derives from 'bard' meaning 'poet'.

  Robert, son of Waldave de Biggar, granted a Charter to Richard Baird of Meikle and Little Kyp in Lanarkshire in the thirteenth century. The surname appears in the fourteenth century in Aberdeenshire and in the Lothians.

| PLACES of INTEREST | | |
|---|---|---|
| **GRAMPIAN** | | |
| BANFF AND BUCHAN | *Auchmeddan,* 3 miles NW of New Aberdour, was owned by the Baird family, and was bought by the Earl of Aberdeen when, as prophesied by Thomas the Rhymer, the eagles which nested in the crags, disappeared. They returned after the marriage of the heir to General Baird's sister and remained until the estate again passed out of the family, when they departed. | |
| **STRATHCLYDE** | | |
| DUNBARTON | *Helensburgh.* Birthplace of John Logie Baird. | |
| GLASGOW CITY | *Strathclyde University.* There is a plaque to former student John Logie Baird, the television pioneer, in Cathedral Square. | |

# Barclay

Of Norman origin, the surname derives from Roger de Berkeley as does that of the English Berkeleys from Berkeley Castle, Gloucestershire. They settled in Scotland in the twelfth century.

Sir Walter Barclay of Gartly, Lord of Redcastle and Inverkeillor, was Chamberlain of Scotland under William the Lion. The male line of Gartly ended with Walter, Canon of Moray in 1456. His sister married the Laird of Towie-Barclay and thus carried the chiefship into that house.

Field marshal Michael Andreas Barclay was commander of the Russian Army which defeated Napoleon in 1812. He was created Prince Barclay de Tolly.

| PLACES of INTEREST | GRAMPIAN | |
|---|---|---|
| | GORDON | *Gartly* is situated 5 miles S of Huntly. Ruins of twelfth-century castle. *Urie,* SE of Huntly. Lands owned by David Barclay in the seventeenth century. |
| | BANFF AND BUCHAN | *Towie Barclay Castle,* sixteenth-century. Can be seen A947 road from Old Meldrum to Macduff. Restored as residence, 1970. No admission. |

# Borthwick

The name is of Celtic origin, and is held by a prominent Border family. A Borthwick accompanied Queen Margaret to Scotland in 1061; another rescued his Scottish host from the Saracens and captured back the heart of Robert Bruce. The first Lord Borthwick was a hostage for James I.

| **PLACES of INTEREST** | **BORDERS**<br>ROXBURGH | *Borthwick Water,* flows into the River Teviot. Barony name taken from this area. |
| | **LOTHIAN**<br>MIDLOTHIAN | *Borthwick Castle,* near Fushiebridge, off A7. Built by 1st Lord Borthwick in 1430. Bothwell brought Mary Queen of Scots here after their wedding. Not open to the public. *Crookston,* Heriot. Seat of Head of Family. No admission. |

Borthwick Castle

# Boswell

An Ayrshire family. James, the biographer of Dr Samuel Johnson, was born in Edinburgh in 1740 where his father Lord Auchinleck, was a Court of Session judge.

| | | |
|---|---|---|
| **PLACES of INTEREST** | **STRATHCLYDE** CUMNOCK AND DOON VALLEY | *Auchinleck House,* Auchinleck, beside River Lugar, off A76. There are ruins of two keeps, the second of which is said to date from 1612. The Barony Kirk houses a Boswell Museum. Open Easter–September. |

# Boyd

The family was well established in Ayrshire before the reig
of Robert Bruce. The Lordship of Boyd was created in 145
and William, 10th Lord, became Earl of Kilmarnock in
1661. Thomas Boyd was created Earl of Arran in 1467, bu
was forfeited.

| PLACES of INTEREST | STRATHCLYDE | |
|---|---|---|
| | KILMARNOCK AND LOUDOUN | *Dean Castle,* Kilmarnock. Seat of Lords of Kilmarnock. Restored by Lord Howard de Walden and gifted t the town of Kilmarnock in 1975. Ope to the public all the year round. |

# Boyle

The family of De Boyville came from Normandy with William the Conqueror. The Welsh branch were ancestors of the Earls of Cork and Shannon.

Hugo de Morville, a cousin of the De Boyvilles, came to Scotland and became Hereditary Great Constable under David I. About 1140, he made over the lands of Kelvin to the De Boyvilles. The male line died out in 1196, and passed through a daughter to the Earls of Galloway. This male line failed in 1234. The Earldom of Glasgow was created for David, Lord Boyle in 1703.

| PLACES of INTEREST | STRATHCLYDE | |
|---|---|---|
| | CUNNING-HAME | *Kelburne Castle,* Fairlie, off A78. Held by ancestors of the Earls of Glasgow since reign of Alexander III. Grounds open to public as Kelburne Country Park, May–September. |

# Brodie

One of the original Pictish tribes of Moray. The name comes from the Barony of Brodie. Records were destroyed when Brodie House was burned in 1645 by Lord Lewis Gordon.

It is known that Michael, Thane of Brodie, held a Charter from Robert Bruce about 1311, erecting the old Celtic Thaneage into a Barony.

| PLACES of INTEREST | HIGHLAND MORAY | |
|---|---|---|
| | | *Brodie Castle,* Forres. Erected 1609 incorporating old fortalice. Seat of Chief. Owned by National Trust for Scotland. Open to the public. |

# Bruce

The Norman family of de Bruis came to England with William the Conqueror in 1066. They received lands in Yorkshire, and Robert de Bruis, through his association with David I of Scotland, obtained the Lordship of Annandale in 1124.

Robert, 5th Lord, married Isabella of Huntingdon, second daughter of the Earl of Huntingdon and great-granddaughter of David I, and their son was nominated one of the Regents of the Kingdom of Scotland, and a guardian of Alexander III in 1255. In 1290, after the deaths of Alexander III and his granddaughter and heiress, the Maid of Norway, this same Robert claimed the crown of Scotland as nearest heir. King Edward I of England over-ruled this claim in favour of John Baliol, who was the grandson of the elder daughter of the Earl of Huntingdon.

Sixteen years later, Robert Bruce asserted the claim again, the throne having fallen vacant through Baliol's renunciation. The royal Bruce line was taken up by the Stewart descendants of Lady Marjory Bruce, his daughter.

From the Bruces of Clackmannan, cousins of King Robert, descend the Earls of Elgin, a title conferred in 1633 on Thomas, 3rd Lord Bruce of Kinloss.

| PLACES of INTEREST | | |
|---|---|---|
| | **BORDERS** ETTRICK AND LAUDERDALE | *Melrose.* The heart of Robert Bruce was brought to the Abbey here after the Crusades. It is buried under the altar. |
| | **CENTRAL** CLACK-MANNAN | The tower here is the ancient fortalice of the Bruces of Clackmannan. |

STIRLING

*Bannockburn.* The battlefield where Robert Bruce won his great victory in 1314. His monument stands next to the Rotunda. Lord Elgin, descendant of the Bruce family, lent his support to the efforts to conserve this area, and to the setting up of the monument.

**DUMFRIES AND GALLOWAY**

ANNANDALE AND ESKDALE

*Dumfries.* There is a plaque on the site of Greyfriars' Kirk, commemorating Bruce's stabbing of Comyn the Red which began the fight for independence.

*Lochmaben Castle,* ancient fortress of the Bruces of Annandale.

|  |  |
|---|---|
|  | *Lockerbie* — Kirkpatrick Fleming, the cave in which Robert Bruce is said to have hidden, and where he supposedly met the spider which inspired him to try again. |
| WIGTOWN | *Glen Trool.* A stone marks the site of an early victory by Bruce over a band of English troops. |

**FIFE**

| DUNFERMLINE | The remains of Robert Bruce are interred in the Abbey Church of *Dunfermline* (except his heart — see Borders).
*Broomhall* is the seat and family home of the Earl of Elgin and Kincardine, Head of House of Bruce. |
|---|---|

**TAYSIDE**

| PERTH AND KINROSS | *Scone.* Robert Bruce crowned King of Scots here in 1306, after his murder of John Comyn the Red in Dumfries. |
|---|---|

# Buchan

Associated with Clan Cumming, the Buchans consider themselves a separate clan. They are the old 'tribe of the land'. The district extending from the Don to the Deveron was a province under the rule of a Pictish Mormaer, and the Earldom of Buchan emerged in the twelfth century. The Comyns, on marrying the heiress, did not take the name and arms, and the tribe continued under its own chief.

---

**PLACES of INTEREST**

**GRAMPIAN**
GORDON

*Auchmacoy,* near Ellon. Buchan chief holds this Barony.
*Earl's Mount,* Ellon. Site of mediaeval motte where justice was administered by Earls of Buchan.

---

# Buchanan

A Stirlingshire clan of Pictish origin whose lands were on the east side of Loch Lomond. They are said to have descended also from an Irishman called Anselan O'Kyan, who settled in the Lennox in the eleventh century.

In the thirteenth century, Gilbert, Seneschal to the Earl of Lennox, obtained a Part of the Lands of Buchanan and took his name from them. The principal line became extinct in 1762 and the Buchanan lands were sold to Graham of Montrose. The Buchanan line gradually dwindled and dispersed — one Buchanan of Ulster Scots descent became the 15th President of the USA. But in 1753, the Buchanans legally incorporated their name, septs and branches; this, the oldest clan society, registered arms in 1919.

**LACES of NTEREST**

**CENTRAL**
STIRLING

*Ardoch,* Strathyre. Birthplace of Dugald Buchanan (1716-85). Gaelic poet and evangelist.
*Clairinch* (nature reserve), Loch Lomond. Island owned by Buchanan Society, and from which derives clan slogan. The island was gifted to the Buchanans in 1225.
*Moss,* Strathblane. Birthplace of George Buchanan (1506-82), notorious tutor to James VI.

**pts**

Colman, Donleavy, Dove, Dow, Findlay, Finlayson, Gibb, Gibson, Gilbertson, Harper, Harperson, Lennie, Lenny, MacAldonich, MacAndeoir, MacAuselan, MacAslen, MacCalman, MacCalmont, MacChruiter, MacCormack, MacGibbon, MacGilbert, MacGerusick, Macinally, MacIndeoir, MacIndoe, Mackinlay, MacMaster, MacMaurice, MacMurchie, MacNuyer, MacWattie, MacWhirter, Masterson, Murchie, Murchison, Risk, Ruskin, Spittal, Spittel, Watson, Watt, Yule, Yuill.

# Cameron

The Gaelic name, Cam-shron, means crooked nose, and relates to an early chief. The clan consisted of the MacMartins of Letterfinlay, the MacGillonies of Strone and the MacSorleys of Glen Nevis. The original possessions were confined to the portion of Lochaber lying on the east side of the loch and river of Lochy, held of the Lord of the Isles as superior. Through all the struggles with the English the Camerons staunchly upheld the Stuart cause: Cameron of Lochiel lent his support to Bonnie Prince Charlie, and heavily influenced early Jacobite victories.

In 1793 Cameron of Erracht raised the 79th Highlanders — later named the Queen's Own Cameron Highlanders. Cameron lands were the west side of Loch Lochy: Glen Loy and Loch Arkaig, Glen Kingie, Glen Dessary, Glen Pean and Glen Mallie, and Mamore further south.

## PLACES of INTEREST

### GRAMPIAN
GORDON

*Brux,* woods seen across River Don after Bridge of Alford. Here a feud between Camerons and Mowatts was to have been settled between 12 horsemen from either side. The Mowatts appeared with two men on each horse and massacred the Camerons.

### HIGHLAND
LOCHABER

*Achnacarry,* near Loch Arkaig. Seat of Cameron of Lochiel. Built in the nineteenth century, it stands beside the castle burned by Cumberland in 1746. No admission.

*Annat,* Loch Eil. Ancient home of the Cameron chiefs.

*Fort William.* West Highland Museum Cameron Square. Exhibition and relics on history of Lochaber.

*Kilmallie.* An obelisk commemorates Col. John Cameron of Fassfern who fell at Quatre Bras (1815).

*Lochan a' Chlaidherich* (Little Loch of the Sword), near Rannoch Station. Here Ewen, 17th Chief, met the Earl of Atholl on disputed ground.

Gormsuil, a witch, had forewarned Lochiel of treachery and when Atholl signalled his hidden warriors to appear, Lochiel signalled to his. Atholl, realising his ploy had failed, renounced his claim to the land and tossed his sword into the lochan.

## TAYSIDE
PERTH AND
KINROSS

*North Inch,* Perth. Scene of the celebrated 'battle of the clans' in 1396, between the champions of Clan Chattan and those of Clan Kay (perhaps Cameron).

**Septs**

Chalmers, Clark, Clarkson, MacChlerich, MacClery, MacGillorie, MacIldowie, MacKail, MacMartin, MacOnie, MacSorley, MacUalrig, MacUlric, Martin, Martyne, Paul, Sorley, Taylor.

# Campbell

Breadalbane

Loudoun

Cawdor

Argyll

Sir Colin Campbell of Lochawe was recognised by the King of Scotland in 1292 as one of the principal barons of Argyll. The name is derived from the Gaelic 'Cam-beul' or 'crooked mouth', and the Gaelic clan name is 'Clann na Duibhne', which derives from a Diarmid O'Duine of Lochawe.

Sir Colin's son, Sir Neil, was a staunch supporter of Robert Bruce, and was awarded extensive grants of land. The Campbells of Strachur claim descent from Sir Colin's brother, and from his younger son came the Campbells of Loudoun. From a younger son of Sir Neil came the Campbells of Inverawe. The Campbells of Glenorchy (Breadalbane) extended Campbell influence eastwards until it embraced Loch Tay; they became Earls of Breadalbane in 1677, Marquesses in 1831. The Breadalbanes added to their possessions to the detriment of Clan Gregor. Eventually the Chief of Glenorchy could travel from the east end of Loch Tay to the coast of Argyll without leaving his own land.

Muriel, daughter of the 7th Thane of Cawdor, married Sir John Campbell, 3rd son of Argyll, in 1510. When she died, she settled the Thanedom on her grandson, John; hence the Campbells of Cawdor.

In the mid-fifteenth century the Campbells of Lochawe became Earls of Argyll. As the power of the MacDonald Lords of the Isles declined, the Campbells benefited. Argyll acquired Knapdale and Kintyre, and the last great acquisition of land took place in the late seventeenth century when Mull, Morven, Coll and Tiree were added to Argyll lands, wrested from the bankrupt Macleans. The titles in the grant of 1701 by which the Earl of Argyll was created a Duke reflect clan territory at its greatest extent — 'Duke of Argyll, Marquess of Kintyre and Lorn, Earl Campbell and Cowal, Viscount Lochow and Glenyla, Lord Inveraray, Mull, Morvern and Tiree'. He was, in addition, Heritable Sheriff of Argyll and Grand Master of the Household in Scotland and Keeper of the castles of Dunstaffnage, Tarbert and Dunoon.

**PLACES of INTEREST**

**CENTRAL**

CLACK-
MANNAN

*Castle Campbell* (Castle Gloom), near Dollar. Acquired by the Earl of Argyll in the fifteenth century. Sixty acres of woodland cared for by the National Trust for Scotland.

**GRAMPIAN**

MORAY

*Cawdor Castle,* near Nairn. Acquired in middle ages. Seat of the Earls of Cawdor. Old Central Tower is fifteenth-century. Open to the public.

**STRATHCLYDE**

ARGYLL AND
BUTE

*Ardchattan Priory,* Loch Etive. The Campbell-Preston family who own these lands are descended from the last Prior of Ardchattan, a Campbell of Cawdor.

*Carnasserie Castle* (sixteenth-century). On A816. Walls almost complete. Held by Campbells of Auchinbreck.

*Carrick Castle,* Loch Goil. Originally Lamont, but passed to Campbell.

*Crarae.* On A83. Seat of Campbells of Succoth.

*Dunstaffnage.* Former MacDougall castle awarded to Sir Colin and placed in the hands of a Constable, Sir Arthur Campbell.

*Innis Chonnel,* Loch Fyne — castle belonged to Sir Colin Campbell of Lochawe.

*Inveraray.* 1st Earl moved here in 1457. Castle is headquarters of the Clan Campbell Society.

*Kilchurn Castle,* Loch Awe. Erected by Sir Colin Campbell of Glenorchy in 1440. (No admission, but can be seen from the A85.)

KYLE AND
CARRICK

*Loudoun Hall* (sixteenth-century), Ayr. Acquired by the Campbells of Loudoun; restored by the Marquis of Bute and gifted to the Saltire Society.

OBAN

*Tobermory Bay,* Isle of Mull. A grea
ship of the Spanish Armada sank her
in 1588. Rights of salvage granted t
the Earl of Argyll by Charles I.

**TAYSIDE**
PERTH AND
KINROSS

*Black Castle,* near Moulin on A924 N
of Pitlochry. Robert Bruce granted
lands to Sir Colin of Lochawe.
*Taymouth Castle,* Kenmore. Origina
castle built by Sir Colin of Glenorch
in 1580. Now a college. No admissior
*Edinample Castle,* Loch Earn (seventeenth-century). Built by Sir Duncar
of Glenorchy on the site of the forme
Clan Gregor stronghold. No
admission.
*Finlarig Castle,* near Killin (sixteenth
century). Seat of the Campbells of
Glenorchy. Parliament summoned t
meet here in 1651, but only three
members turned up.

**Septs**

Arthur, Bannatyne, Burnes, Burness, Burnett, Burns, Caddell, Cadel, Calder
Cattell, Connochie, Conochie, Denoon, Denune, Gibbon, Gibson, Harres,
Harris, Hastings, Hawes, Haws, Hawson, Isaac, Isaacs, Iverson, Kellar, Keller
Kissack, Kissock, Lorne, Loudon, Louden, Loudoun, Lowden, Lowdon,
MacArtair, MacArthur, MacCarter, MacConachie, MacConchie,
MacConnechy, MacConnochie, MacDermid, MacDermott, MacDiarmid,
MacEller, MacElver, MacElvie, MacEver, MacGibbon, MacGlasrich,
MacGubbin, MacGure, MacIsaac, MacIver, MacIvor, MacKellar, MacKelvie,
MacKerlie, MacKessack, MacKessock, MacKissock, MacLaws, MacLehose,
MacNichol, MacNocaird, MacOnachie, MacOran, MacOwen, MacPhedran,
MacPhun, MacTause, McTavish, MacUre, Moore, Muir, Ochiltree, Orr,
Pinkerton, Taweson, Tawesson, Thompson, Torrie, Torry, Ure.

# Carnegie

The name derives from the lands of 'Carryneggy' or Carnegie in Angus, confirmed by David II on John de Balinhard in 1358. The direct line of the Carnegies of that Ilk expired in 1563 and from Duthac de Carnegie, 2nd son of John, derives the House of Southesk. Sir David Carnegie was created Earl of Southesk by Charles I in 1633: The estates and title were forfeited after the Jacobite rising of 1715, but they were later recovered. The Earldom of Northesk was assumed in 1666 by John, younger brother of the 1st Earl of Southesk, and previously Earl of Eathie. The most famous latter-day Carnegie was multi-millionaire Andrew Carnegie from Dunfermline.

**LACES of NTEREST**

**FIFE**
DUNFERMLINE Cottage in Moody Street *Dunfermline* is birth place of Andrew Carnegie, the nineteenth-century steel tycoon who did much to benefit Scotland. Memorial Museum.

**HIGHLAND**
SUTHERLAND *Skibo Castle,* SW of Dornoch. Bought by Andrew Carnegie and still owned by his family. Montrose was taken here after his capture in 1650. No admission.

**TAYSIDE**
ANGUS *Kinnaird Castle,* Brechin. Built by family who acquired lands in the fifteenth century. The castle was rebuilt in the nineteenth century, and enlarged by Bryce. Seat of Earl of Southesk. No admission.
*Farnell Castle,* Brechin. Acquired by the Carnegies in 1623. Now an old people's home.

# Charteris

Francis, 2nd son of Earl of Wemyss succeeded to estates and peerage when his elder brother, Lord Elcho, was attainted for his part in the '45 Rising. He took the name and arms of Charteris of Amisfield under entail. The Wemyss Estate and arms, however, devolved to the 3rd son of the 5th Earl, as James Wemyss of Wemyss.

| PLACES of INTEREST | | |
|---|---|---|
| | **BORDERS** | |
| | TWEEDDALE | *Neidpath Castle,* Peebles on A72. Currently owned by Wemyss Estates. Open April–October. |
| | **DUMFRIES AND GALLOWAY** | |
| | NITHSDALE | *Amisfield,* 5 miles NE of Dumfries. Belonged to Charteris family from the thirteenth century. Tower dates from 1600. |
| | **LOTHIAN** | |
| | EAST LOTHIAN | *Amisfield Estate,* Haddington, formerly a seat of the Earl of Wemyss, presented to town and now a golf course. *Gosford House,* Aberlady. Seat of Earl of Wemyss and March. No admission. |
| | **TAYSIDE** | |
| | PERTH AND KINROSS | Lands of *Kinfauns* near Kinnoul Hill, given by Robert Bruce to Thomas de Longueville, who founded the family of Charteris. Passed to Carnegies, then Blairs. Present castle dates from 1822. Ruins of *Elcho Castle* (1530) — on south side of River Tay — open to public. |

# Chattan
## (Tribal Federation)

The name of this Clan comes from Gillichattan Mór, the 'Great Servant of St Catan' of the ancient Culdee Church, who lived on Bute. By the twelfth century, the descendants of the Saint's family and followers had spread to Glenloy and Locharkaig in Lochaber. In the 7th generation Eva, an only child, married Angus, 6th of Mackintosh in 1291. They were compelled to flee from Lochaber for safety, and settled in Rothiemurchus where the Mackintoshes had already been established for 150 years. From this time dates the emergence of the great Clan Chattan confederation.

In time the clans 'of the blood' of the old Clan Chattan — Macpherson, Cattanach, MacBean, MacPhail, Mackintosh, Shaw, Farquharson, Ritchie, and MacThomas — were joined by other clans seeking protection — Macgillivray, Davidson, Maclean of Dochgarroch, Macintyre in Badenoch, Macqueen, Gow and Clark.

For nearly five centuries, the Clan Chattan was a force to be reckoned with, holding lands which extended from Inverness to Laggan in the Upper Spey Valley.

---

**PLACES of INTEREST**

**HIGHLAND**

| | |
|---|---|
| BADENOCH AND STRATHSPEY | *Aviemore,* Rothiemurchus old Church. Grave of Shaw Mór, traditional leader of 30 Clan Chattan champions at Perth. |
| LOCHABER | *Mulroy,* near Roy Bridge. Last clan battle took place here in 1688. |

**STRATHCLYDE**

| | |
|---|---|
| ARGYLL AND BUTE | Priory of *Ardchattan* on Loch Etive was consecrated in honour of Gillichattan Mór. |

**TAYSIDE**

| | |
|---|---|
| PERTH AND KINROSS | *North Inch,* Perth. Clan Battle fought between 30 champions of Clan Chattan and 30 from Clan Kay or possibly, Clan Cameron, 1396. |

---

# Chisholm

Found in Roxburghshire and originally spelled De Chesholm. The original Border seat was the Barony of Chisholme; the later line of Scott-Chisholme died out in 1899.

In the fourteenth century, Alexander de Chesholm, son of Sir Robert de Chisholme, Constable of Urquhart Castle, married Margaret, Lady of Erchless, daughter and heiress of Wyland of the Aird. Their son, Thomas de Chisholm, born 1403, is forebear of the Chisholms of Comar and Strathglass, later called 'Chisholm of Chisholm'.

| | | |
|---|---|---|
| **PLACES of INTEREST** | **BORDERS** ROXBURGH | *Chisholme,* near Hawick. Original seat of the family. |
| | **HIGHLAND** INVERNESS | *Corriedoe,* Glenmoriston. The cave in which Prince Charles Edward sheltered with the seven men of Glenmoriston, three of whom were Chisholms. *Erchless,* Strathglass. Former seat of Chisholms. No longer owned by Chief. No admission. *Urquhart Castle,* Loch Ness. Robert de Chisholm, founder of the northern line of the Chisholm clan, married the daughter of the Constable of Urquhart Castle, and in turn, became Constable himself in the fourteenth century. |

# Cochrane

Name taken from 'Five-Merk' land of Cochrane (Coueran), near Paisley in Renfrewshire. Waldeve de Cochrane witnessed a charter in favour of the 5th Earl of Menteith in 1262. The family was raised to the peerage in 1647.

A traditional military family, but Archibald, 9th Earl of Dundonald was a scientist and inventor, and Thomas, 10th Earl, served in the Royal Navy and later commanded the Chilean, Peruvian, Brazilian and Greek navies in the nineteenth century.

| PLACES of INTEREST | STRATHCLYDE | |
|---|---|---|
| | KYLE AND CARRICK | *Dundonald*, Kyle, on A759. Castle of Stewarts twelfth-thirteenth centuries. Estates bought by Cochranes in the seventeenth century. It is now a ruin. *Auchans*, Kyle. Ruins of castellated mansion built by 1st Earl of Dundonald. |
| | RENFREW | Lands of *Cochrane* held by family, later Earls of Dundonald. *Place of Paisley*, Paisley. Town house of Earls of Dundonald after 1653. Open to the public. |

# Cockburn

Name derived from a place near Duns, Berwickshire. They were ancient vassals of the Earls of March and ancestors of Cockburns of Langton, Ormiston and Clerkington. David II conferred the Barony of Carriden in West Lothian on Sir Alexander de Cockburn and Alexander Cockburne was Keeper of the Great Seal. Admiral Cockburn conveyed Napoleon to St Helena.

| PLACES of INTEREST | | |
|---|---|---|
| | **BORDERS** | |
| | TWEEDDALE | *Skirling* held by family. Castle demolished in 1568 because they supported Mary, Queen of Scots. |
| | **LOTHIAN** | |
| | EDINBURGH | *Bonaly Tower,* home of Lord Cockburn, nineteenth-century judge and antiquary. Now converted into flats. |
| | EAST LOTHIAN | *Ormiston Estates* owned by Adam Cockburn (1656–1735). |
| | WEST LOTHIAN | *Carriden,* Bo'ness. Barony conferred on Sir Alexander. |

# Colquhoun

A territorial name taken from the Barony of Colquhoun in Dunbartonshire. The founder of the family was Humphrey de Kilpatrick or Kirkpatrick, who obtained a grant of the lands in the reign of Alexander II. Lands of Luss acquired during late fourteenth century by marriage to the 'Fair Maid of Luss', a descendant of Maldwin, Dean of the Lennox in 1150.

**PLACES of INTEREST**

**STRATHCLYDE**

DUNBARTON

*Dumbarton Castle,* Dumbarton. Off A814. Sir John Colquhoun of Luss was Governor under James II.
*Glenfruin.* Tragic defeat of Alexander, 12th Laird of Luss with 200 Colquhouns by MacGregors, 1603. The MacGregors were outlawed for the act.
*Inchmurrin Castle,* Inchmurrin, Loch Lomond. Island castle where Sir John Colquhoun was murdered with his attendants, 1439. It is now a ruin.
*Luss,* on East shore of Loch Lomond. Lands held since the fourteenth century.
*Rossdhu,* Luss, on A82. Seat of chiefs. Open April–September.

**Septs**

Cowan, Kilpatrick, Kirkpatrick, MacCowan.

# Cumming, Cumin or Comyn

Descended from a Norman noble, Richard Cumyn, the Cummings became powerful in Scotland. In reign of Alexander III, Atholl, Buchan and Menteith were Cumming earldoms. By marriage with the sister of King John Baliol, and by descent from King Duncan, John, Lord of Badenoch — the 'Red Comyn' — had a strong claim to the Scottish throne. After the confrontation with Robert Bruce where 'Red Comyn' was killed, the family declined.

The Comyns of Altyre took over the chiefship and through marriage with the Gordons of Gordounstoun, the name Gordon-Cumming was adopted.

| PLACES of INTEREST | | |
|---|---|---|
| | **CENTRAL** STIRLING | *Inchmahome,* Lake of Menteith (beside A873). Isle of St Colmoc. Priory founded for Austin Canons c.1238 by Walter Comyn, Earl of Menteith. Open April–November. Admission fee includes ferry. |
| | **DUMFRIES AND GALLOWAY** DUMFRIES | *Dumfries.* Church of the Greyfriars. Red Comyn stabbed by Robert Bruce, 1306. (A plaque marks the spot.) |
| | **GRAMPIAN** BANFF AND BUCHAN | *Balvenie Castle,* Dufftown. A941. Fourteenth-century moated stronghold of Comyns. Substantial ruin. On River Fiddich. *Deer Abbey,* inland from Peterhead. B2029. Founded 1219 by Comyn, Earl of Buchan, for Cistercian Monks from Kinloss. Now ruined. |
| | LOCHABER | *Inverlochy Castle,* Fort William, off A82. The thirteenth-century castle was built for the Comyns. There are substantial remains; the modern castle nearby is an hotel. |

| MORAY | House of *Blair-of-Altyre*. 4 miles S of Forres. Seat of Chief. No admission. *Lochindorb,* off A939. Island stronghold built by Comyns in the thirteenth century. In 1372 the notorious 'Wolf of Badenoch', son of Robert II, used Lochindorb as the centre for his terrorising activities. |

**HIGHLAND**

| INVERNESS | *Urquhart Castle,* Loch Ness. Held by Comyns. Open to public. |
| NAIRN | *Rait Castle,* 2½ miles S of Nairn. Scene of the massacre of the Comyn chiefs by the Mackintoshes. |

**STRATHCLYDE**

| WIGTOWN | *Cruggleton Castle,* Garlieston. B7063. Massive thirteenth-century fortalice, held by Comyns, but little now remains. |

epts    Buchan, Commyn, MacNiven, Niven, Russell.

Balvenie Castle

# Cranston

This family descends from Elfric de Cranston, a Norma
who lived in the twelfth century. The Cranstons owne
lands in Edinburgh and Roxburghshire. Lordship created
1609.

| **PLACES of INTEREST** | **BORDERS** ROXBURGH | *Melrose Abbey*, Cranston family tombs.<br>*Craeling*, Roxburgh. Cranston monument. |
|---|---|---|
| | **LOTHIAN** MIDLOTHIAN | *Cranston* (Cranstoun–Riddell), situat SE of Dalkeith.<br>*Cranston Parish Church*, off A68, is policies of Oxenfoord Castle. Built 1824. |

# Crawford

## See Lindsay

Surname derived from Barony of Crawford in the Upper Ward of Clydesdale. In 1248, Sir John of that Ilk died leaving two daughters, of whom the eldest married Archibald de Douglas, and the younger married David Lindsay of Wauchopedale, ancestor of the Earls of Crawford and Balcarres. A cadet branch produced Sir Archibald of Loudoun, the Sheriff of Ayr murdered at a banquet by the English. His sister married Sir Malcolm Wallace of Elderslie, and was mother to the patriot.

| PLACES of INTEREST | STRATHCLYDE | |
|---|---|---|
| | KILMARNOCK AND LOUDOUN | *Kilwinning,* off A760. Kilbirnie Place, fourteenth century. Crawford seat burned in the eighteenth century. *Loudoun Estates* on River Irvine originally owned by Crawfords, but carried to Campbells through marriage. Loudoun Hall open mid July-end October. |
| | TAYSIDE | |
| | PERTH AND KINROSS | *Glendevon Castle,* among Ochil Hills. Castle held by Crawfords in the sixteenth century, now ruined. No admission. |

# Cunningham

The family descends from Warnibald, who settled in the district of Cunningham, Ayrshire, in the twelfth century. Harvey de Cunningham received the lands of Kilmaurs from Alexander III after Battle of Largs 1263. Alexander de Cunningham was created Earl of Glencairn by James III in 1488, and was later killed at the Battle of Sauchieburn.

| PLACES of INTEREST | DUMFRIES AND GALLOWAY | |
|---|---|---|
| | NITHSDALE | *Maxwellton House,* Moniaive, off A702. Part of house, famous as birth place of Annie Laurie, dates back to fourteenth–fifteenth centuries when the Earls of Glencairn had a stronghold here. Open May–September. |
| | STRATHCLYDE | |
| | KILMARNOCK AND LOUDOUN | *Kerelaw Castle,* Stevenston, belonged to the Earls of Glencairn. Sacked by the Montgomeries of Eglinton in the fifteenth century. *Kilmaurs,* near Kilmarnock — burgh of barony for Earl of Glencairn, 152 |

# Dalzell

Barony of Dalzell in Lanarkshire gives origin to this name. A kinsman of King Kenneth II, so it is said, was hanged and the king offered a great reward to the man who could rescue the body. A man stepped forward and exclaimed 'Dal Zell' which in old Scots means 'I dare'. The family had lands in Lanarkshire and Dumfriesshire, and a cadet branch built the House of Binns in West Lothian.

Sir Thomas Dalyell of the Binns (1599-1685) raised the Royal Scots Greys Regiment in 1681 — it is now called the Royal Scots Dragoon Guards.

Variant spellings are Dalyell, Dalzel, Dalziel and Dalziell.

---

**PLACES of INTEREST**

**LOTHIAN**

MIDLOTHIAN — *Rullion Green,* Carnethy Hill, beyond Flotterstone Bridge, off A702. Battle won in 1666 against Covenanters by General Tam Dalyell.

WEST LOTHIAN — *Abercorn Church,* on Hopetoun Estate, near South Queensferry, 2 miles N of A904. Although legend has it that General Tam's body was taken by the Devil, his tomb is in the churchyard here.

*The House of the Binns,* near Linlithgow, off A904. Part of the house dates from 1478. Property owned by the National Trust for Scotland. Open Easter–September.

---

The Binns

53

# Davidson

### See Clan Chattan

Donald Dubh of Invernahavon, Chief of the Davidsons
married a daughter of Angus, 6th of Mackintosh and soug
protection of William, 7th of Mackintosh before 1350 an
became associated with Clan Chattan Confederation. Th
clan became known as Clan Dhai.

The Davidsons maintained a consistent feud with the
Macphersons regarding precedence within Clan Chattan
The famous 'battle of the clans' fought on the North Inch i
Perth (1396) possibly fought by Davidsons (Clan Dhai o
Kay) and the Macphersons in an attempt to settle this issue

The main families were the Davidsons of Cantray in
Inverness-shire and the Davidsons of Tulloch in Ross-shir

| PLACES of INTEREST | HIGHLAND | |
|---|---|---|
| | NAIRN | *Cantray,* on River Nairn, 9 miles N of Inverness. |
| | | *Castle of Tulloch*, 1 mile N of Dingwal Dates from the fifteenth century. |
| | ROSS AND CROMARTY | *Dingwall Castle,* Dingwall. Thirteentl century castle, now in ruins. Chief ( Clan Davidson was Hereditary Keeper. |

| Septs | Davie, Davis, Dawson, Dow, Kay, MacDade, Macdaid, MacDavid. |
|---|---|

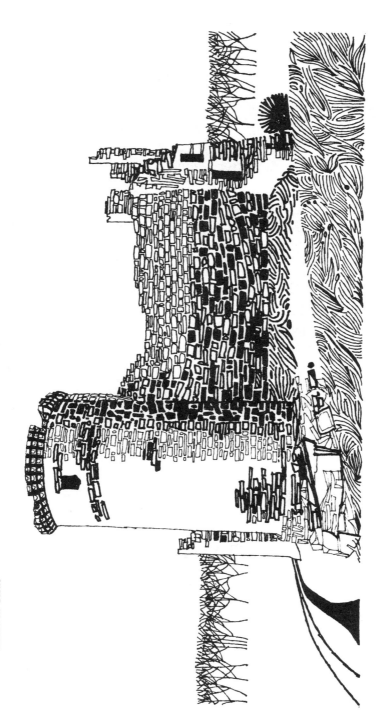

Bothwell Castle

55

# Douglas

The first recorded of this name is William de Douglas, who lived in the twelfth century. Grants of land were made to Sir James Douglas, one of Bruce's chief lieutenants. At one time they were the most powerful family in Scotland. Because of their strength, the Douglases were a constant threat to the Scottish throne, and their title and estates were forfeited in 1455. These Douglases were ancestors of the Earls of Morton, Douglas, Annandale, Moray, Ormond, Angus and Forfar, and the Dukes of Touraine, Queensberry and Buccleuch, and Hamilton.

In 1761, the Duke of Hamilton became Earl of Angus and heir-male to the Douglas Estates. After litigation (The Douglas Cause), the heir-female was recognised as representing the House of Douglas and was awarded the Chief Arms. These were carried by her daughter into the family of the Earls of Home.

---

**PLACES of INTEREST**

**BORDERS**
ROXBURGH

*Blackhouse Tower,* on Douglas Burn by Yarrow Water. Stronghold of James the Good, friend of Robert Bruce.
*Hermitage Castle,* N. of Newcastleton, off A6399. The fourteenth-century stronghold of Douglases. Later owned by Earl of Bothwell. Open to the public.

**CENTRAL**
STIRLING

*Stirling Castle.* William, 8th Earl of Douglas murdered here by King James II, 1452.

**DUMFRIES AND GALLOWAY**
NITHSDALE

*Drochil Castle,* near Biggar, off A72. Erected by Regent Morton in 1570. Now ruined. No admission.
*Drumlanrig,* near Thornhill, off A76. Lands confirmed 1412 by James I. In the seventeenth century, Douglas of Drumlanrig rose to be Duke of Queensberry. On death of the 3rd Duke, the title passed to the Earls of

**STEWARTRY OF KIRKCUD-BRIGHT**

March, and in 1810 to Dukes of Buccleuch. Open April–August.
*Castle Douglas.* Originally called Carlingwark and re-named by eighteenth-century merchant, William Douglas.
*Threave Castle,* Castle Douglas, N of A75. Built in fourteenth century by Archibald the Grim, Lord of Galloway, 3rd Earl of Douglas. Open all year.

**FIFE**

**DUNFERMLINE**

*Aberdour Castle,* Aberdour on A92. Fourteenth-century castle held by Douglas, Earls of Morton. Burned accidentally in the eighteenth century. Ruined. Open to public.
*Aberdour Nunnery,* founded in 1486 by 1st Earl of Morton.

ntallon

| | |
|---|---|
| **NORTH-EAST FIFE** | *Lindores Abbey,* Lindores, near Newburgh, off A913. The 9th Earl of Angus was confined here by the Duke of Albany in the fifteenth century. Ruined. |

## LOTHIAN

| | |
|---|---|
| EAST LOTHIAN | *Tantallon Castle,* near North Berwick on A198. Held by Douglas Earls of Angus. Almost impregnable castle on cliff top. Cromwell's General Monck was first to take Tantallon in 1651, after twelve days of bombardment. Fell into decay after 1699. Open to public. |
| EDINBURGH | *Edinburgh Castle.* Old Parliament Hall. The boy 6th Earl of Douglas and his brother were murdered here in 1440 in front of the 8 year old King James II. The deed was instituted by Chancellor Crichton to break Douglas power. |
| MIDLOTHIAN | *Mortonhall Country Club.* Seat of Earl of Morton (near Ratho). |

## STRATHCLYDE

| | |
|---|---|
| HAMILTON | *Bothwell Castle,* Uddingston, on A74. Built by Lords of Bothwell in the thirteenth century and held by Douglases from 1362-1859. Now ruined. Open to the public. |
| LANARK | *Douglas.* Burgh of Barony under Douglas Earls of Angus, 1459. Burgh of Regality under Duke of Douglas, 1707. |

## TAYSIDE

| | |
|---|---|
| PERTH AND KINROSS | *Blackfriars Monastery,* Perth. James I murdered here in 1437 despite the bravery of Catherine Douglas, who thrust her arm through the staples of the door in place of a missing iron. *Glendevon Castle,* Glendevon. Held by Douglases in the fifteenth century. *Loch Leven Castle,* Loch Leven, off M90. Property of Sir William Douglas of Loch Leven when Mary, Queen of Scots was held here (1567-68). Open May-October. |

# Drummond

The surname derives from the lands of Drummond or Drymen in Stirlingshire. Malcolm Beg, Steward of the Earldom of Strathearn in 1255 is the first recorded, and his son, Sir Malcolm took the name Drummond. Margaret Drummond married King David II in 1364, and Annabella Drummond married King Robert III.

The Barony was created in 1488. The 4th Lord was created Earl of Perth in 1605. The younger brother of the 3rd Lord Drummond was created Lord Madderty, and from him descends the Viscount of Strathallan.

The Drummonds supported the Stuarts and followed the fortunes of James VII who created them Dukes of Perth and Dukes of Melfort. Both lines became extinct and succession passed to the House of Strathallan. The old Drummond estate passed, through an heiress, to the Earls of Ancaster.

| PLACES of INTEREST | | |
|---|---|---|
| | **CENTRAL**<br>STIRLING | *Dunblane Cathedral,* Dunblane, on A9. Margaret Drummond, daughter of 1st Lord Drummond is buried here. She was poisoned with her sister, allegedly because she was an obstacle to King James IV's marriage to Margaret Tudor. |
| | **TAYSIDE**<br>PERTH AND KINROSS | *Drummond Castle,* 3½ miles S of Crieff, off A8022. Built in 1491. Destroyed by Jacobite Duchess of Perth, 1745. Modern house added. Now seat of Earl of Ancaster. Gardens open April-October, Wednesdays and Sundays. *Megginch Castle,* Carse of Gowrie, on A85. Held by Drummonds. Gardens open April-June and September, Wednesday; July-August, Monday and Friday. *Stobhall,* 8 miles N of Perth. Four-teenth-century castle, Seat of Earl of Perth. No admission. |

Grewar, MacGrowther, Macgruder, Macgruther, MacRobbie.

# Dunbar

Crinan the Thane and Seneschal of the Isles was father of King Duncan I and of Maldred, whose son Cospatrick became Earl of Northumbria in 1067. In 1072, he was deprived of that Earldom by William the Conqueror, and coming to Scotland in refuge, was given the Earldom of Dunbar by King Malcolm III.

Cospatrick's descendant, Patrick, 8th Earl, was also Earl of March. The 9th Earl married Agnes, daughter of Thomas Randolph, 1st Earl of Moray. Agnes achieved renown for her spirited defence of Dunbar Castle in 1338. On the death of her brother, she inherited the title. Having no issue at her death, the Dunbar Earldom devolved to John, the son of her sister Isobel Randolph. He became Earl of Moray in 1372, and married Marjorie, daughter of King Robert II.

The poet William Dunbar (1460–1520) is supposed to have been from near Dunbar in East Lothian.

| PLACES of INTEREST | | |
|---|---|---|
| | **DUMFRIES AND GALLOWAY** WIGTOWN | *Mochrum.* Land owned by Dunbars, and later, MacDowalls. Castle owned and restored by Bute family. |
| | **HIGHLAND** MORAY | *Elgin Cathedral,* Elgin. 'Bloody Vespers' — scene of murderous brawl between Dunbar and Innes families in 1555. |
| | **LOTHIAN** EAST LOTHIAN | *Dunbar Castle,* Dunbar. Held by Earl of Dunbar since Cospatrick. Defended by 'Black Agnes' against English in 1338. Only ruins remain. |
| | **STRATHCLYDE** CUMNOCK AND DOON VALLEY | *Cumnock.* Belonged to Dunbar Earl of March and held until the seventeenth century. |

# Duncan
### see Clan Donnachaidh (Robertson)

Descended from ancient Earls of Atholl and took name from a chief Donnachaidh, or 'Fat Duncan' who led the clan at Bannockburn. The Robertson appellation derives from their chief, Robert, in the time of James I. Considered as a Sept of Clan Donnachaidh. The Duncans possessed lands in Forfarshire including the barony of Lundie and Estate of Gourdie.

| PLACES of INTEREST | TAYSIDE | |
|---|---|---|
| | DUNDEE | *Lundie,* NW of Dundee. Barony held by Duncans. |
| | PERTH AND KINROSS | *Gourdie,* Murthly. Estate once held by Duncans. No admission. |
| | | *Rannoch* — Duncan's Leap on the River Ericht. 'Duncan the Fat', a follower of Robert Bruce, leapt across here after reconnoitering the MacDougall camp. |

# Dundas

Serle de Dundas is recorded in the reign of King William the Lion. The Dundases were a great Lowland family playing a prominent part in the legal affairs of the Nation dating from Sir James, Lord Arniston (d. 1679).

The statesman Henry Dundas, 1st Viscount Melville, was known as the 'uncrowned king of Scotland'. Dundas was 'manager' of Scotland for William Pitt, and President of Board of Control for India. Through his influence many Scots found lucrative openings in that country. Also through his offices were many forfeited estates restored, and the ban on the wearing of the tartan lifted.

| PLACES of INTEREST | | |
|---|---|---|
| | **LOTHIAN** | |
| | EDINBURGH | *St Andrew Square* — Royal Bank of Scotland. Built in 1772, and designed by Chambers as town house of Sir Lawrence Dundas. Lost by him in a poker game. In St Andrew Square Garden rises the Melville Monument, topped by a statue of Henry Dundas by Forrest, 1828. |
| | MIDLOTHIAN | *Arniston House,* Gorebridge. Built for the Dundas family, who had held lands here since 1571. (Privately owned.) *Melville Castle,* NE of Lasswade. Built by Playfair (1786) on site of previous castle. Home of Henry Dundas, 1st Viscount Melville. Passed to him through marriage. Now a hotel. |
| | WEST LOTHIAN | *Dundas Castle,* 1½ miles SW of South Queensferry. Originally built by James Dundas of that Ilk in 1424. Privately owned. *Inchgarvie.* Island in the Forth garrisoned by Dundas family in fifteenth century for protection of shipping. Surrendered to Cromwell. |
| | **TAYSIDE** | |
| | PERTH AND KINROSS | *Dunmore Hill,* 1 mile N of Comrie. Obelisk in memory of Lord Melville (1724–1811). |

# Elliot

A family of Southern Scotland. They were one of the great
'riding' clans of the Borders. Elliots of Redheugh were
recognised as principal family. The current Chiefly line of
Elliot of Stobs originated in the sixteenth century. A
descendant of the Stobs family founded the Minto family,
later Earls of Minto.

| PLACES of INTEREST | BORDERS | |
|---|---|---|
| | ROXBURGH | *Hermitage Castle.* Several Elliots were captains of the castle. |
| | | *Minto House,* near Hawick. Seat of Earl of Minto. No admission. |
| | | *Redheugh,* Newcastleton. Seat of Chief. No admission. |
| | | *Stobs,* near Hawick. Former seat of Chief. No admission. |

# Erskine

The name derives from the Barony of Erskine in Renfrewshire. This was held by Henry de Erskine in the reign of Alexander II. Sir Thomas de Erskine married Jan Keith, grand-daughter of Lady Eline de Mar, and their son Robert, became heir to one of the oldest Celtic earldon and chief of the ancient 'tribe of the land' of Mar. Rober 4th Lord Erskine was killed at the battle of Flodden, and hi son James, 5th Lord, was father of the Regent. In 1565 Joh 6th Lord, was restored as Earl of Mar by Mary, Queen Scots, who was also held to have created a new Earldom Mar. This has caused much confusion since the mid eighteenth century. The Earldom of Mar and Kellie is currently held by the chief of the clan. The ancient Earldom of Mar is held by another family.

In 1715 John Erskine, Earl of Mar, led the Jacobite Risin and was attainted and his estates forfeited: another Jacobit Lord Lyon Sir Alexander Erskine of Cambo, was mere imprisoned.

Braemar Castle

**PLACES of INTEREST**

**CENTRAL**

CLACK-
MANNAN

*Alloa Tower.* Fourteenth-century. Once stronghold of Earls of Mar and, at times, childhood home of Mary, Queen of Scots.

STIRLING

*Cambuskenneth Abbey,* 1m NE Stirling. Founded by King David I in 1140. Erected in 1604 as a Lordship for John, Earl of Mar. Free standing tower remains. Open to public.

*Mar's Wark,* Stirling. Remains of a town house built by the Regent Mar in 1570. Open all times.

**FIFE**

NORTH EAST
FIFE

*Cambo,* Crail. Seat of Erskines of Cambo. No admission.

*Kellie Castle,* near Pittenweem, off A921. Fourteenth-century. Acquired by Thomas Erskine in 1613. He was 1st Earl of Kellie and slew Ruthven in so-called Gowrie Conspiracy. Open Good Friday–September. National Trust for Scotland.

Dirleton
Castle

## GRAMPIAN

**KINCARDINE AND DEESIDE**

*Braemar Castle,* Braemar, on A93. Built in 1628 by John, Earl of Mar (1562–1634) to dominate his vassals th Farquharsons. Open May–October. *Braes of Mar.* John, Earl of Mar, raise the standard for the Old Pretender i 1715.

## LOTHIAN

**EAST LOTHIAN**

*Dirleton Castle,* Dirleton, on A198. Owned by Sir John Erskine of Goga in the seventeenth century.

**CITY OF EDINBURGH**

*Edinburgh Castle,* Edinburgh. John, Earl of Mar (1510–72), keeper durin revolution (1559–60).

## TAYSIDE

**PERTH AND KINROSS**

*Cardross,* Menteith. Tower house hel by Erskines. No admission. *Inchmahome Priory.* A81. Temporal Lordship for John, Earl of Mar, 1604

# Farquharson
## See Clan Chattan

Farquhar, son of Alexander Ciar, 3rd Shaw of Rothiemurchus, was the originator of the clan. His descendants settled in Aberdeenshire, and Farquhar's son, Donald, married Isobel Stewart, heiress of Invercauld. Their son Finlay Mor, 1st of the House of Farquharsons of Invercauld, was killed at the Battle of Pinkie in 1547.

Many Farquharsons were Jacobites, and fought at Prestonpans and Culloden.

---

**PLACES of INTEREST**

**GRAMPIAN**
KINCARDINE AND DEESIDE

*Braemar Castle,* Braemar, A93. Built by the Earl of Mar in 1628. Passed to Farquharsons in 1732.
*Cairn na Cumline* (Cairn of Remembrance), 2 miles SW of Balmoral. Rallying place of the Farquharsons.
*Invercauld House,* Braemar. Seat of the Chief. No admission.

---

**Septs**

Coutts, Farquhar, Findlay, Findlayson, Grevsach, Hardie, Hardy, Leys, Lyon, MacCaig, MacCardney, MacEaracher, MacFarquhar, MacGruaig, MacHardie, MacKerrachar, Mackinlay, Reach, Riach.

---

# Fergusson or Ferguson

The first settlement of this clan would appear to have been at Kintyre. Kilkerran, the seat of the Fergusson chiefs in Ayrshire (now generally acknowledged as chief of the name), is the modern Gaelic form of the name Campbeltown, and is named after St Ciaran, one of the twelve apostles of Ireland who landed at Dalruadhain in the sixth century.

The Fergussons of Kilkerran descend from Fergus, son of Fergus in the time of Robert Bruce. Fergus, King of Galloway in the reign of David I, married a daughter of Henry I of England. The Fergussons of Craigdarroch in Dumfriesshire have a recorded history that dates back to a charter from David II in the fourteenth century. Other Fergussons lived in Atholl; their chief was Dunfallandy, and the family can be traced back to the fifteenth century. The poet, Robert Fergusson, who was much admired by his young contemporary, Robert Burns, presented a copy of his verses to Kilkerran, his chief.

| | | |
|---|---|---|
| **PLACES of INTEREST** | **DUMFRIES AND GALLOWAY** | |
| | WIGTOWN | *Soulseat Abbey,* Lochinch. Founded by Fergus of Galloway. |
| | **GRAMPIAN** | |
| | BANFF AND BUCHAN | *Peterhead* — Deer Abbey, on A950. Site bought in 1809 by Ferguson family. Admiral Ferguson virtually destroyed the remains of the Abbey Church to build a mausoleum on the site. |
| | **LOTHIAN** | |
| | EDINBURGH | *Holyrood,* Edinburgh. Fergus, Lord of Galloway died here in 1161. |
| | **STRATHCLYDE** | |
| | KYLE AND CARRICK | *Kilkerran House,* S of Maybole. Seat of Chief. No admission. |

# Fletcher

This name means 'arrow maker', and therefore is found all over Scotland. The Fletchers followed the clans for which they made arrows. In Argyll, they are associated with the Stewarts and the Campbells, in Perthshire, with the MacGregors. In the sixteenth century, the Fletchers entered into a bond with Campbell of Glenorchy. They possessed Achallader for generations.

Andrew Fletcher of Saltoun (1653-1716), was a Member of Parliament. He opposed the Duke of Lauderdale and Duke of York (later James VII). He was exiled, but returned at time of William and Mary, and was famous as a leading anti-unionist.

| PLACES of INTEREST | **LOTHIAN** | |
|---|---|---|
| | EAST LOTHIAN | *Saltoun,* Haddington. Purchased by Fletcher family 1643. |
| | **STRATHCLYDE** | |
| | ARGYLL AND BUTE | *Achallader Castle,* Glen Tulla. Home of Fletcher family before Glenlyon Campbells. The plot for the massacre of Glencoe is said to have been conceived here. |

# Forbes

The Clan Forbes is said to originate from Ochonochar, who slew a bear and won the up–until–then uninhabitable Braes of Forbes in Aberdeenshire. His family settled there and a Charter of 1271 altered the tenure to feudal. Alexander de Forbes was one of the fiercest opponents of King Edward I of England and lost his life defending the Castle of Urquhart on Loch Ness. The first Lord Forbes, created a Peer in 1445, married a granddaughter of Robert III.

| | | |
|---|---|---|
| **PLACES of INTEREST** | **GRAMPIAN** BANFF AND BUCHAN | *Cave of Cowshaven,* Aberdour Bay. Alexander, last Lord Pitsligo, a Jacobite who fought at Culloden aged 68, was concealed here by his friends. *Corgarff Castle,* Strathdon, off A939. In 1571, during the feud between the Gordons and Forbes, Corgarff was defended by wife of the absent Alexander Forbes. The tower was set on fire and rather than surrender, its defender, her children and household perished. Ruin was rebuilt as barracks by Government in eighteenth century. It can be seen from road. Open to the public. *Pitsligo Castle,* Pitsligo. Ruins date back to 1424. Keep built by Sir William Forbes. Now a ruin. |
| | GORDON | *Castle Forbes,* Alford. Nineteenth-century seat of Lord Forbes. No admission. *Colquhonnie Castle,* Strathdon. Begun by Forbes of Towie in the sixteenth century. Never completed. Now a ruin. *Craigievar Castle,* Alford, N of junction of A974 and A980. Built in 1626 for a Forbes laird 'Danzig Willie' who was a merchant. National Trust for Scotland. Open May–September. *Druminnor,* near Rhynnie, off A97. Fifteenth-century tower of Lords of |

Forbes with 1577 mansion incorporated. Open Sundays in summer.
*Monymusk.* Augustinian Priory mentioned in 1245. Passed to Forbes family. Sixteenth-century tower. Sold in 1713.
*Pitfichie Castle,* near Monymusk. Sixteenth-century. Owned by Forbes of Monymusk in seventeenth century.
*Tolquhon Castle,* Old Meldrum, off B999. Through marriage passed to Forbes family in sixteenth century. Open all year.

KINCARDINE AND DEESIDE
*Corse Castle,* A947, in the grounds of Corse House. Belonged to Patrick Forbes, Bishop of Aberdeen. Said to have been visited by the Devil who carried off the front of the house. No admission.

**HIGHLAND**
INVERNESS
*Culloden House,* Culloden, on B9006. Eighteenth-century. Duncan Forbes, Laird of Culloden, was Lord President of the Court of Session at the time of the 1745 uprising.

Septs    Bannerman, Fordyce, MacQuattie, MacWatt, Michie, Watson, Watt, Watters.

# Forsyth

Robert de Fauside signed the Ragman Roll in 1296. Later Forsyth chiefs became members of the Royal Stewart Household at Falkland, and their arms are shown in early sixteenth-century Armorials. At the time of Cromwell, however, the name disappeared and the family scattered.

| | | |
|---|---|---|
| **PLACES of INTEREST** | **FIFE** NORTH-EAST FIFE | *Falkland Palace,* on A912. Sixteenth-century Royal Residence. National Trust for Scotland. Open April–October. |

Falkland Palace

| | |
|---|---|
| **TAYSIDE** ANGUS | *Ethie Castle,* Brechin. Built by Cardinal Beaton. Home of current chief. No admission. |

# Fraser

Frasers appeared in Scotland in the twelfth century — a Simon Fraser gave lands to the monks of Kelso in 1160.

The main line develops from Sir Gilbert of Touch-Fraser, Stirling, who died in 1263. Sir Alexander, 8th of Philorth, finding himself in financial difficulties when expanding his town and University of Fraserburgh (Aberdeenshire), disposed of the Manor of Philorth. Fraser of Muchalls acquired the 'undifferenced' arms and named his estate Castle Fraser. In 1633, he became Lord Fraser. The Chiefship is held by the Earldom of Saltoun.

Sir Alexander of Philorth's younger brother, Simon Fraser, who fought for Robert Bruce, is believed to be the forebear of the branch of the family which acquired the Lordship of Lovat by marriage to a daughter of the Earl of Orkney and Caithness. From Simon, the chief of Clan Lovat is called *MacShimi*, 'son of Simon'. In 1815, the direct line failed and Fraser of Strichen, a cadet of the Lovat family, became Chief of the Frasers of Lovat.

---

**PLACES of INTEREST**

**CENTRAL**
STIRLING

*Touch,* 2 miles W of Stirling, belonged to Bernard Fraser, Sheriff of Stirlingshire in 1234. It was known as Touch-Fraser. In the hands of the Seton family from the sixteenth century.

**GRAMPIAN**
BANFF AND BUCHAN

*Cairnbulg Castle,* near Inverallochy (seen from B9033). Comyn stronghold acquired by Frasers. The castle was renovated in the late nineteenth century. Seat of Chief. No admission. *Fraserburgh.* University founded in 1542 by Sir Alexander Fraser of Philorth. Survived for 10 years.

GORDON

*Castle Fraser,* Kemnay. Built by Michael Fraser (d. 1588) and his son. National Trust for Scotland. Open May-September.

**HIGHLAND**
INVERNESS

*Beaufort Castle,* Beauly. Nineteenth-century mansion. Seat of Frasers of Lovat. No admission.

**LOCHABER** *Neck between Loch Lochy and Loch Oich.* In July 1544, clan battle between Frasers and Macdonalds — Battle of the Shirts — so called because clansmen discarded their plaids.

# Gair

The House of Gayre arose in Cornwall before the thirteenth century from the Great Doomsday Manor of Gayre. In time the senior line became extinct and the second line migrated to Yorkshire and became involved in the destruction of a castle which forced them to flee to Scotland.

They married into the Mowes of Mowe and later, into the MacCullochs of Nigg, a branch of the MacCullochs of Plaids, custodians of the Girth of St Duthac, Tain, a noted mediaeval shrine venerating the eleventh-century chief confessor of Ireland and Scotland.

| PLACES of INTEREST | | |
|---|---|---|
| **HIGHLAND** | | |
| ROSS AND CROMARTY | | *Nigg.* Ancestral lands. Now centre of oil developments with large platform construction yard. |
| **STRATHCLYDE** | | |
| ARGYLL AND BUTE | | *Minard Castle,* Loch Fyne, off A83. The current chief has declared that the *Duthus* of the clan is here since the developments on the ancient lands make that location unsuitable. At Minard Castle there are records, a library, a small armoury and a portrait gallery. Viewed by arrangement: telephone Minard 272. |

septs      Gair, Gaire, Gayer, Gayre, Geare, Geere, Laing, MacRobbie, Norris, Parker.

# Galbraith

Clan connected with Earls of Lennox, through Clan Macfarlane. At one time, branch took protection of Clan Donald. The clan was known as *Chlann a' Bhreatannaich* — children of the Britons — and are connected with the island of Gigha.

| PLACES of INTEREST | CENTRAL STIRLING | *Balgair Castle,* Fintry. Adjoins Culcreuch, but now a ruin. *Culcreuch Castle,* Fintry. Owned by clan by 1320. Extended to a fortified keep in 1460 and in 1721 extensively added to. Privately owned, but open to the public. *Inchgalbraith,* Loch Lomond. Ruins of Gilchrist "Bhreatnach's" fort can still be seen, although level of loch has risen and less of island is visible. |
| --- | --- | --- |

# Gordon

The earliest record of the name Gordon in Scotland was in the late twelfth century, relating to the parish of Gordon in the Merse in Berwickshire.

Adam de Gordon was an Anglo-Norman, and was with King Louis XI of France in the Crusades of 1270. Under Robert Bruce, Sir Adam, Lord of Gordon, acquired the Lordship of Strathbogie in Banffshire. He died at the Battle of Halidon Hill in 1333.

His great-grandson died at the Battle of Homildon in 1402, leaving a daughter, Elizabeth, as heiress. She married Sir Alexander Seton, second son of Sir William Seton of Seton, and their son was created Earl of Huntly in 1449. George, 6th Earl, defeated Argyll in 1592 and became Marquess in 1599. Dukedom granted in 1684. In 1836, the 5th Duke died without issue and George, 9th Marquess of Huntly became Chief of the name.

The Gordons of Haddo, created Earls of Aberdeen in 1682, are descended from Patrick Gordon of Methlic, who fell at the Battle of Arbroath in 1445. John Gordon of Glenbuchat, known as 'Old Glenbucket', was a staunch Jacobite; active in both the risings of 1715 and 1745, he was forced to flee to Norway after Culloden, and died abroad. John, 7th Earl and 1st Marquess of Aberdeen was Governor General of Canada.

---

**PLACES of INTEREST**

**BORDERS**
BERWICKSHIRE  *Gordon* Village is SW of Greenlaw.

**GRAMPIAN**

KINCARDINE AND DEESIDE  *Aboyne Castle,* seat of the Marquess of Huntly. At the annual Aboyne Highland Gathering, one of the most important of such meetings in Scotland, the banner of the chief of the Clan Gordon is prominent on display.

GORDON  *Glenbuchat Castle,* Glenbuchat, off A97. The sixteenth-century Gordon tower can be seen from the road. May be viewed from the outside.

*Gordon Castle,* near Fochabers off Aberdeen/Inverness road (A96). Seat of the Duke of Richmond and Gordon. The ancient tower of the Earls of Huntly, fifteenth- to sixteenth-century, known as Bog of Gight Castle, rises behind the present mansion.

*Haddo House,* 6½ miles NW of Ellon off B9005. Seat of the Marquesses of Aberdeen and Temair. National Trust for Scotland. Open to the public, May–September.

*Huntly Castle,* Huntly. Splendid ruin formerly known as Strathbogie Palace, former seat of the Gordons.

| Septs | Adam, Adie, Crombie, Edie, Huntly, Milne, Todd. |
|-------|--------------------------------------------------|

# Gow or Macgowan
## See Clan Chattan

Gow is the Gaelic 'Gobha', meaning blacksmith. Generally regarded as sept of Clan Chattan and closely connected with the MacPhersons, but all clans had blacksmiths.

Henry of the Wynd, a smith from Perth, fought for the Macphersons in the battle of the North Inch.

| Septs | MacGowan, Smith. |
|-------|------------------|

# Graham

The first Graham appears to be William de Graham, alive in the twelfth century, although 'Gramus' who demolished the wall of defence built by the Roman Emperor Antoninus is said to be originator. King David I gave William the lands of Abercorn and Dalkeith. His descendants acquired the Lordships of Kinnaber and Old Montrose in 1325. Sir William Graham married Mary, 2nd daughter of Robert III. Patrick, their eldest grandson became Lord Graham, then Earl of Montrose in 1504. James, 5th Earl was the celebrated 1st Marquis, and James, 4th Marquis was created Duke of Montrose.

Another member of the clan was John of Claverhouse, Viscount Dundee, the 'Bonnie Dundee', persecutor of Covenanters and staunch Jacobite campaigner, hero of Killiecrankie.

| | | |
|---|---|---|
| **PLACES of INTEREST** | **CENTRAL** STIRLING | *Kilsyth*. Battle in 1645 at which 5th Earl gained victory over Covenanters, killing 6000 and losing only 10 of his own men. Exhibits on view at Colzium, a mansion 1 mile NE, now a community centre. *Mugdock*, 2 miles N of Milngavie. Lands acquired by David de Graham. Castle dates from the thirteenth century. No admission. |
| | **HIGHLAND** SUTHERLAND | *Ardvreck Castle*, Assynt, off A837. Ruin of fifteenth-century Macleod castle at which the Marquis of Montrose was captured and held after Carbisdale. *Carbisdale*, near Bonar Bridge on A836. Here Marquis of Montrose made his final stand for Charles II in 1650 and was defeated. |
| | **LOTHIAN** CITY OF EDINBURGH | *St Giles' Cathedral*, Edinburgh. Beneath the floor of the Chapman Aisle are the remains of 1st Marquis of |

Montrose, whose monument is on the east wall.

## STRATHCLYDE

**CUNNING-HAME**

*Brodick Castle,* Isle of Arran. Original castle held by Edward I. Passed to Montrose family through marriage with daughter of 12th Duke of Hamilton. National Trust for Scotland. Open Easter–September.

## TAYSIDE

**ANGUS**

*Old Claverhouse Castle,* Dundee. Site marked by a Dovecot. Here 'Bonnie Dundee', John Graham of Claverhouse, was born.

*Old Montrose.* Birthplace of James, 5th Earl and 1st Marquis of Montrose. (1612–1650).

**PERTH AND KINROSS**

*Braco Castle,* 1½ miles NW Braco on A822. Seat of the Graham family in the seventeenth century (cadets of Earls of Montrose). It passed from the family at the end of the eighteenth century. No admission.

*Killiecrankie,* 3 miles SE of Blair Atholl on A9. Battle at which 'Bonnie Dundee' was killed in 1689. Visitor centre (National Trust for Scotland).

*Kincardine Castle,* near Auchterarder. Seat of Graham Earls of Strathearn. Passed to Grahams of Montrose. Original castle dismantled by Argyll in 1645. New mansion is nineteenth-century. No admission.

# Grant

A main branch of the 'Siol Alpine' of which Clan Gregor is chief. The originator of the Grants is said to have been Gregor Mór MacGregor, who lived in the twelfth century in Strathspey. Sir Lawrence Grant, Sheriff of Inverness in 1263 is first recorded ancestor.

**PLACES of INTEREST**

**HIGHLAND BADENOCH AND STRATHSPEY**

*Ballintomb,* near Dulnain Bridge on A939. Rallying place of the clan. *Castle Grant,* N of Grantown-on-Spey. Sixteenth-century. Name changed in the seventeenth century from Freuchie. Seat of Earls of Seafield after the Earldom was acquired through marriage of 20th chief to Lady Margaret Ogilvie.

Castle Urquhart

| | |
|---|---|
| | *Craigellachie,* near Aviemore. Clan lands began here. |
| | *Duthill,* on road from Carrbridge to Grantown-on-Spey. Twin Grant mausoleums can be seen. |
| | *Grantown-on-Spey* on A939 — formerly Castletoun-of-Freuchie. Town planned by Sir James Grant of Castle Grant in 1776. |
| INVERNESS | *Urquhart Castle,* near Drumnadrochit, on Loch Ness. James IV gifted the castle to John Grant of Freuchie in 1509, who built most of the structure seen today. Grants held Urquhart for 400 years despite part being blown up in 1691 to deny Jacobite access. |
| MORAY | *Cullen House,* Cullen. Home of the Earls of Seafield. Dates from the sixteenth century. No admission. |

**Septs**      Gilroy, MacGilroy, Maciaran, MacIlroy, MacKerran.

# Gunn

Believed to be descendants of Guinn, 2nd son of the Norwegian Olave the Black, the King of Man and the Isles who died in 1237. The clan originates from Caithness and Sutherland and they were enemies of the Keiths.

| PLACES of INTEREST | HIGHLAND CAITHNESS | *Clan Gunn Museum,* N of Latheron on A9, N of junction with A895. *Clyth,* 2 miles E of Lybster. Ancient Gunn stronghold. *Harpsdale,* 8 miles S of Thurso. Scene of a particularly bloody conflict between Keiths and Gunns in 1426; however, the battle was indecisive and the feud continued for many years. |
| --- | --- | --- |

**Septs**

Eanrig, Enrich, Gainson, Gallie, Georgeson, Henderson, Jameson, Johnson, Kean, MacCorkill, MacIan, MacKaimes, Mackeamish, MacRob, MacWilliam, Manson, Nelson, Robson, Sandison, Swanson, Williamson, Wilson.

# Guthrie

The name is probably derived from 'Guthrum', a Scandinavian prince. In 1299, it was Squire Guthrie who brought Sir William Wallace back to Scotland from France.

The Barony of Guthrie was granted by King David II. Sir David Guthrie was King's Treasurer in the fifteenth century.

| | | |
|---|---|---|
| **PLACES of INTEREST** | **LOTHIAN** EDINBURGH | *The National Museum of Antiquities,* Queen Street. The Guthrie Bell, believed to date from the eighth century. |
| | **TAYSIDE** ANGUS | *Guthrie Castle,* Friockheim, near Forfar. Built by Sir David Guthrie in 1468. House built about 1760 and connected to the tower in 1848. |

# Haig

A Border family first noted in the thirteenth century with Petrus de Haga. Haigs fought at Halidon, Otterburn and Flodden.

| | | |
|---|---|---|
| **PLACES of INTEREST** | **BORDERS** ETTRICK AND LAUDERDALE | *Bemersyde,* near Dryburgh on B6356. Lands held by Haigs in the twelfth century. The sixteenth-century tower forms part of a later mansion. Alienated from family in nineteenth century but presented by the nation to Field Marshal Earl Haig, Allied Leader in the 1914–18 war. No admission. *Dryburgh Abbey,* Dryburgh, off A68. Tomb of Field Marshal Earl Haig. |
| | **LOTHIAN** CITY OF EDINBURGH | *34 Charlotte Square, Edinburgh.* Birthplace of Field Marshal Earl Haig. *Huntly House Museum,* Edinburgh. Relics of Field Marshal Earl Haig. |

# Hamilton

This clan claims descent from Walter Fitz-Gilbert of Hameldone, noted in 1295, and granted lands of Cadzow by Robert Bruce. Lord Hamilton who married James II's eldest daughter was a descendant. The king's grandson became Earl of Arran in 1503, and his grandson, Marquis of Hamilton in 1599. James, 3rd Marquis, was created Duke of Hamilton in 1643. The title passed to his daughter, Anne, who married William Douglas, Earl of Selkirk, later connecting the Dukedom with the Douglas family. Branches include the Dukes of Abercorn and the Earls of Haddington.

---

**PLACES of INTEREST**

**BORDERS**

ROXBURGH

*Mellerstain,* 8 miles W of Kelso, off A6089. Seat of Lord Binning. Built c. 1735 by William Adam for George Baillie. Passed into Haddington family. Open May–September.

**LOTHIAN**

EAST LOTHIAN

*Hamilton House,* Prestonpans. Built by Sir John Hamilton, brother of 1st Earl of Haddington in 1628. National Trust for Scotland. Can be visited by arrangement.

*Lennoxlove,* formerly Lethington, off B6369, home of Maitlands. Bought in the eighteenth century by Lord Blantyre. Seat of Duke of Hamilton. To view: Tel. Haddington 3720.

*Tyninghame,* near East Linton, off A1. Lands granted to 1st Earl of Haddington in 1628. His descendants built Tyninghame House. Seat of Earls of Haddington. Gardens open May–September.

MIDLOTHIAN

*Kinneil House,* near Bo'ness. Sixteenth-seventeenth-century fortified seat of Dukes of Hamilton. Grounds are now a public park.

## STRATHCLYDE

**CUNNING-HAME**

*Brodick Castle,* Isle of Arran. Passed from Hamilton family to Duke of Montrose through marriage. National Trust for Scotland. Open Easter-September. Gardens open all year.

**HAMILTON**

*Cadzow Castle.* Ruins in Hamilton High Park. Seat of the Hamiltons which was destroyed by Earl of Moray after the defeat of Mary, Queen of Scots at Langside.

*Craignethan Castle,* Crossford, A72. Fifteenth-sixteenth-century Hamilton stronghold. The Hamiltons supported Mary, Queen of Scots and castle was dismantled after her flight. A new mansion was built by the Hay family in 1665. Open to the public.

*Strathclyde Regional Park* was formerly known as Hamilton Low Parks, once the park of Hamilton Palace, pulled down 1922-32. The mausoleum in the park was erected by the 10th Duke who died in 1852. It was bought by the town of Hamilton. Open daily except Sunday; telephone Hamilton 24940.

**RENFREW**

*Place of Paisley,* Paisley. (Adjoining church, part of Abbey Buildings). Restored 1956. Owned by the Hamilton family until 1653.

Paisley Abbey

# Hannay

This family sprang from the ancient province of Galloway. The earliest known possessors of Sorbie Tower were the powerful Anglo-Norman family, the Viponts, Lords of Westmorland, who received the manor and lands in 1185. Records of the thirteenth century are sparse, but it is believed that the change of hands to the Hannays could have been through marriage as the family mottos are remarkably similar.

The Hannays supported John Baliol, who by his mother, the Lady Devorgilla, represented the old Celtic Lords of Galloway. In 1308, they were forced to submit to Edward Bruce when he conquered Galloway.

A Gilbert de Hannethes signed the Ragman Roll in 1296. The Hannays rode to Sauchieburn and Flodden; they feuded against or sided with their neighbours the Kennedys, the Dunbars and the Murrays, and joined James IV on his pilgrimages to St Ninian's Shrine at Whithorn. In 1601, the Hannays were outlawed for their behaviour towards the Murrays.

| PLACES of INTEREST | DUMFRIES AND GALLOWAY | |
|---|---|---|
| | WIGTOWN | *Kirkdale,* between Creetown and Gatehouse of Fleet has been the family seat of Hannays of Kirkdale since 1532. House built by Robert Adam. *Rusco Castle,* near Gatehouse of Fleet. In Hannay possession from 1786. Privately owned. *Sorbie Tower,* 7 miles S of Wigtown. Ancient Hannay stronghold until middle of seventeenth century. Restored by Hannay Society. Open to public. |
| | FIFE | |
| | NORTH EAST FIFE | *Kingsmuir Estate,* near Crail. Seat of Hannays of Kingsmuir. |
| epts | Hanna, Hannah, Hannay. | |

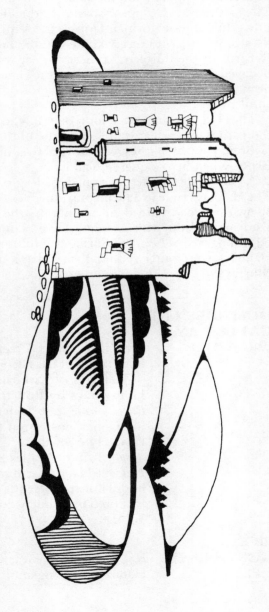

# Hay

There are two accounts concerning the origin of the Hays. The first, traditional one, concerns the Battle of Luncarty believed to have taken place around AD 971. Kenneth III was fighting the Danes and the day was saved by a countryman and his two sons. The king commanded that a falcon be let loose from Kinnoull Hill, and that as far as it flew the lands would belong to the hero and his sons. The bird flew to a stone in St Madoes Parish, taking in some of the best land of the Carse.

The name Hay, however, is documented as dating from the eighth century in France. La Haye de Puits was a senior leader with William the Conqueror and William de Haya was Pincerna (butler) to William the Lion.

William de Haya's son was one of the hostages held in England for the latter king, and, on his return was granted an extensive manor in Erroll. His younger brother, Robert, was progenitor of the Earls of Tweedale.

Sir Gilbert de la Haye, 3rd Lord of Erroll, married Lady Idione Comyn, daughter of William, Earl of Buchan, and sister of the then Lord High Constable of Scotland. Their son, Sir Gilbert, also fought with Bruce and was rewarded with the lands of Slains, near Aberdeen, and the post of Hereditary Lord High Constable, a post which the family still carry.

| | | |
|---|---|---|
| **PLACES of NTEREST** | **BORDERS** | |
| | BERWICKSHIRE | *Duns Castle,* Duns. Keep was built in the fourteenth century by Randolph, Earl of Moray. Estate came to Hays of Drumelzier in seventeenth century. No admission. |
| | TWEEDDALE | *Haystoun House,* Peebles. Earliest part sixteenth-century. No admission. *Neidpath Castle,* near Peebles, on A72. Raised in thirteenth century. Visited by Mary, Queen of Scots and James VI. Defended against Cromwell. Now owned by Wemyss Estates. Open April–October. |

## DUMFRIES AND GALLOWAY

WIGTOWN

*Park Castle, Glenluce,* off A75. Built by Thomas Hay of Park, son of last Abbot of Glenluce in 1596. Said to have been built from stones of the Abbey. No admission.

## GRAMPIAN

BANFF AND BUCHAN

*Delgatie Castle,* Turriff, off A947. Sixteenth-century. Clan Hay Centre To view, telephone Turriff 3479. *Leith Hall,* Inverurie, B9002. Home of the Leith–Hays, National Trust for Scotland. (Open May–September.)

Neidpath Castle

| | |
|---|---|
| GORDON | *Slains Castles* (old and new), off A975. Ruins. Johnson and Boswell stayed at New Slains. Open to public. |

## LOTHIAN

| | |
|---|---|
| EAST LOTHIAN | *Yester Castle,* near Gifford, erected in 1268 by Hugo de Gifford, ancestor of the Hays of Yester. Sir Walter Scott mentions it in Marmion, but it is currently owned by the Ministry of Works. No admission.<br>*Yester House,* home of the Marquesses of Tweeddale, was occupied by 1704; but the work by William and Robert Adam continued. It was sold by the widow of the 11th Marquess for tax reasons and is now privately owned. No admission. |
| MIDLOTHIAN | *Borthwick Castle.* Early in the thirteenth century, Sir John Hay, great grandson of William de Haya, built the *Mote of Locherwort.* The site was later acquired by the first Lord Borthwick, who built the fine castle of that name on this site. No admission. |

## STRATHCLYDE

| | |
|---|---|
| LANARK | *Craignethan Castle,* near Lanark, on A72. 1665 Hay mansion on ruins of Hamilton stronghold. Open to public. |

## TAYSIDE

| | |
|---|---|
| PERTH AND KINROSS | *Melginch or Megginch Castle,* off A85. Originally a Hay Castle, but owned by Drummonds. Gardens open April-June, Wednesday; July, August, Monday-Friday.<br>*Murie,* 2 miles from Gallowsflat, there is a man made knoll, about 20 feet high, thought to be the original mote of the Erroll family.<br>*Pitfour Castle,* near Perth. Bought by Patrick Hay, a descendant of the Megginch Hays, in the seventeenth-century. Sold in 1809. |

# Henderson or Mackendrick
### Sept of MacDonald of Glencoe

Eannig Mor mac Righ Neachtan, Big Henry, son of King Nectan who ruled Caledonia in the eighth century is said to be the founder of this name. King Nectan was the forebear of the MacNaughtons, and built the pictish tower of Abernethy. The Hendersons held lands encompassing Glencoe and became hereditary pipers of the Clan Abrach. The direct line is believed to have terminated in an heiress, and through marriage, the Hendersons became part of the Macdonald Clan Ian of Glencoe. Their last chief as such was killed at the Massacre of Glencoe.

| | |
|---|---|
| **PLACES of INTEREST** | **FIFE** |
| | DUNFERMLINE *Fordell Castle,* Inverkeithing. Sixteenth-century seat of Hendersons of Fordell. No admission. |
| | **HIGHLAND** |
| | LOCHABER *Glencoe.* The notorious Massacre of Glencoe took place on 13 February 1692. The MacIans of Glencoe were massacred by Campbell of Glenlyon on the instructions of the Master of Stair. MacDonald of Glencoe had delayed until last minute to submit to William and Mary in place of James VII. 128 soldiers who had accepted MacDonald hospitality, turned on their hosts on a given signal. The Glen is now a major centre for rock climbing. National Trust Visitor Centre, open May–October. |
| | **TAYSIDE** |
| | PERTH AND KINROSS *Abernethy.* Ninth-(twelfth) century round tower. Place of refuge. |

# Hepburn

Named for place in Northumberland. For centuries a prominent family in the Scottish Borders, becoming Earls of Bothwell. James, 4th Earl, husband of Mary, Queen of Scots, was forfeited.

**PLACES of INTEREST**

**BORDERS**
ROXBURGH

*Hermitage Castle,* NE of Langholm, off A6399. Thirteenth-century. Exchanged by Earl of Angus for Bothwell Castle by 1st Earl of Bothwell. Forfeited with Earldom. Open all year.

**FIFE**

*St Leonard's College,* St Andrews. Founded by John Hepburn, brother of 1st Earl of Bothwell. He was Prior of St Andrews (d. 1522).

Hailes

## LOTHIAN

EAST LOTHIAN    *Crichton Castle,* SE of Dalkeith. B636?
Fourteenth-century. Current castle
erected by Earl of Bothwell in
sixteenth century. Open to public.
*Hailes Castle,* near Haddington, off
A1. Thirteenth-century in parts.
Passed from Gourlays to Hepburns,
who added tower and walls. Lands o
Hailes granted to Adam Hepburn b
King David II. Bothwell brought
Mary, Queen of Scots here on way
Dunbar. Open all year.
*Nunraw Castle,* near Gifford. Nunner
of Haddington had a fortalice here.
Property passed to Hepburns, then t
Dalrymples. Bought by Cistercian
order in 1946. In 1548, the Scottish
Parliament met here.

MIDLOTHIAN    *Carberry Tower,* 3 miles SE of Musse
burgh: scene of Mary, Queen of Sco
and Bothwell's defeat in 1567. Now
training and conference centre.

## STRATHCLYDE

HAMILTON    *Bothwell Castle,* near Blantyre, on A7
Thirteenth-century. Granted to
Patrick Hepburn, Earl of Bothwell
after 1455. Exchanged with 'Red
Douglases' for Hermitage. Open to
the public.

# Home

Aldan de Home derived his name from the lands of Home in Berwickshire in the twelfth century. His descendant, Sir Thomas, married the heiress of Dunglass. The Barony of Home was created in 1473. Alexander, 6th Lord, was created Earl in 1605. They descend also from Cospatrick, Earl of Dunbar who lived in the thirteenth century.

Lord Home of the Hirsel, former Prime Minister of Great Britain, is a descendant.

| LACES of NTEREST | BORDERS BERWICK | *Dunglass,* 1½ miles NW of Cockburnspath, off A1. Charter to collegiate church granted to Alexander Home 1423. Barony for Lord Home 1489. Open to public. *Fast Castle,* Coldingham, off A1107. Built as a Home stronghold. Possibly thirteenth-century. Ruins accessible, but care should be taken on cliffs. *Hume Castle,* 3 miles S of Greenlaw on B6364. Thirteenth-century ruin, restored in 1794. Once seat of Earls of Home. (Key from caretaker). *The Hirsel,* Coldstream, off A697. Seat of the Earls of Home. No admission to house. Grounds open to the public. |
| --- | --- | --- |

# Hunter

A family who came to Scotland about 1110 from Normandy. Aylmer le Hunter of the County of Are signed the Ragman Roll in 1296. The lands of Hunterston were granted to William Hunter by Robert II in 1374.

| | | |
|---|---|---|
| **PLACES of INTEREST** | **STRATHCLYDE** | |
| | ARGYLL AND BUTE | *Hunter's Quay,* Dunoon. Named after the Hunters of Hafton House nearby who, in the nineteenth century bought up this coastline; now the Royal Clyde Yacht Club. |
| | CUNNING-HAME | *Hunterston,* West Kilbride, off A78. The Atomic Energy Station is situated on lands of Hunterston. Hunterston House, which at the time of publication, still stands, was the seat of the chief. An ancient castle is situated nearby. |
| | GLASGOW | *Hunterian Museum,* University of Glasgow. Museum and Art collection built up by physician William Hunter (1718–83). |

# Innes

Originating in Moray in 1160 in the reign of Malcolm IV when the lands of Innes were given to Berowald — man of Flanders. John Innes was Bishop of Moray and rebuilt Elgin Cathedral after its burning by the Wolf of Badenoch. The Laird of Innes succeeded in 1805 to the Dukedom of Roxburghe.

| | | |
|---|---|---|
| **PLACES of INTEREST** | **BORDERS** ROXBURGH | *Floors Castle,* Kelso, on B6089. Designed by Vanbrugh in 1721. Altered by Playfair a century later. Seat of Duke of Roxburghe. Open early May–late September daily, except Fridays and Saturdays. |
| | **HIGHLAND** MORAY | *Innes House,* Innes, 4 miles NE of Elgin. Lands granted by King Malcolm IV. Held by family until 1767. No admission. |
| Septs | Dinnes, Ennis, Innis, McInnis, McRob, McTary, Marioch, Mavor, Middleton, Mitchell, Oynie, Reidford, Thane, Wilson, Yunie. | |

# Jardine

Du Jardin was a name recorded at the battle of Hastings, an
it is assumed that the family settled in vicinity of Kendal in
the twelfth century, and then moved to Lanarkshire —
Wandel and Hartside area — in the thirteenth century. I
was early in the fourteenth century when they settled in
Dumfriesshire, where they have been ever since.

# Johnstone

A powerful Border clan, they held the central area of
Annandale, and Sir James of that Ilk became Earl of Hartfell
in 1643. The Johnstones were intermittently appointed
Wardens of the West March, alternating in that rôle with the
Maxwells, with whom they had a deadly feud. This was
resolved in 1623. The second Earl became Marquess of
Annandale in 1701. The Earldom is now dormant.

The Johnstons of Aberdeenshire claim descent from
Stiven de Johnston in the fourteenth century.

| PLACES of INTEREST | DUMFRIES AND GALLOWAY | |
|---|---|---|
| | ANNANDALE AND ESKDALE | *Devil's Beef Tub,* A701. Hollow in which Johnstone reivers are said to have hidden their stolen cattle. *Lochwood Tower* near Beattock between A74 and A701. Burned by Maxwells in 1593. |
| | STEWARTRY OF KIRKCUD-BRIGHT | *Dryfe Sands,* Lockerbie. North of Lochmaben Road. Battle in 1593 when Johnstones decisively defeated the Maxwells. |
| | **GRAMPIAN** ABERDEEN | *Caskieben,* Blackburn. Sixteenth-century. Johnston stronghold. Purchased from them by John Keith and now seat of Earl of Kintore (now called Keith Hall). No admission. |

# Keith

One of the most powerful Celtic families. The Hereditary office of Great Marischal of Scotland was held by them from the fourteenth century. For supporting Robert Bruce, they received the lands of Kintore. The Keiths were created Earls Marischal in 1458.

| | | |
|---|---|---|
| **PLACES of INTEREST** | **GRAMPIAN** | |
| | ABERDEEN | *Bank of Scotland,* Marischal Street, Aberdeen. Site of town mansion of 5th Earl Marischal. |
| | | *Benholm Lodging,* Aberdeen. Now known as the Wallace Tower. Built by Sir Robert Keith (brother of 5th Earl Marischal), 1616, as his town house. It has been moved from its original site in Netherkirkgate to Tillydrone Avenue. |
| | BANFF AND BUCHAN | *Peterhead.* Town founded in 1593 by 5th Earl Marischal. Statue in front of Town House is of James Keith, brother of 10th Earl, who became a Marshal in the army of Frederick the Great of Prussia. |
| | | *Inverugie Castle,* N of Peterhead. Sixteenth-century birthplace of Marshal James Keith. Now privately owned (ruin). |
| | GORDON | *Keith Hall Castle,* Inverurie. Earlier called Caskieben. Sixteenth-century. Purchased from the Johnston family by John Keith, Earl of Kintore. Privately owned. |
| | | *Royal Forest of Kintore,* granted to Sir Robert Keith in 1309. *Hallforest* or *Keith Castle* built by Sir Robert. Now a ruin (in private land). |
| | KINCARDINE | *Dunnottar Castle,* S of Stonehaven, off A92. Ancient fortified site mentioned in the seventh century. Oldest part built fourteenth century for Sir William Keith. Scotland's Regalia was brought here for safe keeping in 1651. |

When the castle was besieged by English, they were smuggled out to nearby Church of Kinneff. Lands forfeited 1716. Open May–September.

Dunnottar

# Kennedy

A Galloway Ayrshire family, descendants of Duncan de Carrick who lived in the twelfth century. James of Dunure married May, daughter of King Robert III. Their son, Gilbert, was one of the six Regents of Scotland during the minority of James III. He became Lord Kennedy in 1458. David, 3rd Lord became Earl of Cassilis (1509). Archibald, 12th Earl, became Marquis of Ailsa in 1831. The Kennedys fought at Flodden and at Pinkie, and were involved in a prolonged blood-feud between the Cassilis and Bargany branches of the family.

**PLACES of INTEREST**

**DUMFRIES AND GALLOWAY**

WIGTOWN

*Castle Kennedy.* Built by Earls of Cassilis in 1607. Passed to Earl of Stair. Destroyed in 1716; replaced 1867 by Lochinch Castle, still the seat of the Earl of Stair (not open to the public). Castle Kennedy gardens open mid-April-late September.

**STRATHCLYDE**

KYLE AND CARRICK

*Culzean Castle,* SSW of Ayr. A719. Built by Robert Adam for 10th Earl of Cassilis on site of ancient castle. Seat of chiefs since the fifteenth century. National Trust for Scotland. Park Centre houses information centre. Castle open March-October. Park always open.

*Dunure Castle,* near Culzean. Earl of Cassilis said to have roasted the lay-abbot of Crossraguel in attempt to make him surrender abbey lands in 1570. Now a ruin.

*Maybole Castle,* S of A77. Chapel founded by John Kennedy of Dunure in 1371.

# Kerr

This family originally settled in the Scottish Borders in the fourteenth century. They were probably of Viking descent and came by way of France. Living in the Borders at that time demanded qualities of toughness, courage and wit, and the Kerrs are remembered as Border 'Reivers'. Kerr of Cessford was appointed Warden of Middle March in 1515. Sir Thomas of Ferniehirst supported Mary, Queen of Scots while his cousin, Mark Kerr supported her opponents. Rivalry between the two houses, indeed, raged for very many years, largely over the question of supremacy. Mark's elder brother, Sir Walter of Cessford was ancestor of the Dukes of Roxburghe in the female line of Innes Kerr.

Sir Thomas was created 1st Lord Jedburgh in 1622. Robert, 1st Earl of Ancram, was one of the many Scots who followed James VI to London. Robert (1636-1703) inherited the Ancram peerage from his uncle and the Lothian peerage from his father. He was created 1st Marquis of Lothian in 1701 for services as Justice General of Scotland and High Commissioner to the General Assembly.

| | | |
|---|---|---|
| **PLACES of NTEREST** | **BORDERS** ROXBURGH | *Cessford,* on B6401 to Morebattle. Passed in 1446 to Andrew Kerr, ancestor of Dukes of Roxburghe. Fourteenth-century tower. No admission. *Ferniehirst Castle,* near Jedburgh. Fifteenth-sixteenth-century. Burned by Earl of Sussex, but rebuilt in 1598. Now a Youth Hostel. *Monteviot,* Jedburgh. Home of the Marquess of Lothian, Chief of the name. House and Gardens open May-November. |
| | **LOTHIAN** MIDLOTHIAN | *Newbattle Abbey,* near Edinburgh. Founded by David I. The mansion is seventeenth-century. Gifted to the nation by the 11th Marquess of Lothian. Now a residential college. |

# Lamont

The name is Norse for 'lawman'; the clan was traditionally founded by Ferchar in the thirteenth century. At one time this family owned the greater part of Cowal, but the family seat of Toward was completely destroyed by the Campbells. The clan scattered, but in 1646, Ardlamont became the seat of the chief. A Clan Lamont Society was formed in 1895.

| PLACES of INTEREST | STRATHCLYDE | |
|---|---|---|
| | ARGYLL AND BUTE | *Ascog Castle,* Isle of Bute. Lamont stronghold destroyed by Campbells in 1646. Now a ruin. |
| | | *Dunoon.* Memorial to murdered Lamonts at Castle Hill. |
| | | *Toward Castle,* near Innellan, 4 miles S of Dunoon. Fifteenth-century ruin. Destroyed by the Marquess of Argyll in 1646. Two hundred prisoners brought to Dunoon and murdered. No admission. |

**Septs**

Black, Bourdon, Brown, Burden, Lamb, Lambie, Lamondson, Landers, Lucas, Luke, Lyon, MacAldine, MacClymont, MacGilledow, MacLukas, MacPatrick, MacSorley, Meikleham, Patrick, Sorley, Taylor, Toward, Towart, Turner, White.

# Lauder

This family owned the Bass Rock off the coast of East Lothian in the thirteenth century. Sir Robert de Lauder was Justiciar of the Lothians in 1323. Thomas Lauder (1395–1481) was Bishop of Dunkeld.

| **PLACES of INTEREST** | **BORDERS** | |
|---|---|---|
| | ETTRICK AND LAUDERDALE | *Lauder*. Place from which the name was taken in the thirteenth century. |
| | **LOTHIAN** | |
| | EAST LOTHIAN | *Bass Rock*, 1½ miles out at sea off North Berwick. For centuries owned by Lauder family. Ruin of castle. |
| | EDINBURGH | *Portobello*. Sir Harry Lauder, the famous music hall entertainer was born at 3 Bridge Street in 1870. |
| | **STRATHCLYDE** | |
| | ARGYLL AND BUTE | *Loch Eck*. Glenbranter Estate was once owned by Sir Harry Lauder. Memorial to his wife and son can be seen. |
| | EAST KILBRIDE | *Strathaven*. Lauder Ha' was the home of Sir Harry Lauder at the time of his death. |

The Bass Rock

# Lennox

Alwin MacMuredach MacMaidouern, Mormaer of the Levenach is the first Celtic Earl of this name; he lived in the twelfth century. The 8th Earl, murdered by James I, left three daughters and one illegitimate son.

**PLACES of INTEREST**

**CENTRAL**
STIRLINGSHIRE — *Lennox Castle,* Lennoxtown. Former seat of Lennox of Woodhead family.

**LOTHIAN**
MIDLOTHIAN — *Lennox Castle* (Lymphoy), Currie. Ancient seat of Earls of Lennox. Later owned by George Heriot in late sixteenth century. Now a ruin.

**STRATHCLYDE**
DUNBARTON-SHIRE — The territory of *Levenach* covered most of this country.
*Inchmurrin,* Loch Lomond. On this island there are ruins of Lennox Castle where the Duchess of Albany retired in 1425 after the execution of her husband, her sons and father, the 8th Earl of Lennox.

# Leslie

From the Barony of Lesly in the Garioch. Descent from Bartolf, a Hungarian noble and chamberlain of St Margaret, Queen to Malcolm Canmore, is claimed. By marriage, the Leslies acquired the baronies of Rothes, Fytekill and Ballinbriech. George Leslie of Rothes and Fytekill was created Earl of Rothes in 1457, and John, 6th Earl, Chancellor of Scotland, was created Duke of Rothes in 1680. On his death, the Dukedom became extinct, but the earldom continued through the female line.

Alexander Leslie at one time in command of the Covenanting army was made Earl of Leven in 1641 and David Leslie, routed by Cromwell in 1650, became Lord Newark in 1661.

| **PLACES of INTEREST** | **FIFE** | |
|---|---|---|
| | KIRKCALDY | Leslie lands in *Kirkcaldy* held by family since reign of King Alexander III. *Leslie House* built by Duke of Rothes; burned down 1763. Current house is old people's home. |
| | NORTH EAST FIFE | *Balgonie Castle,* SE from Markinch. Fifteenth-century tower reconstructed by Alexander Leslie, Earl of Leven. Sold in 1824. No admission. *Pitcairlie House,* N of Auchtermuchty. Home of Patrick Leslie, Lord Lindores, 1600. No admission. |
| | **GRAMPIAN** | |
| | GORDON | *Balquhain Castle,* Inverurie. Sixteenth-century ruined tower — ancient seat. *Pitcaple Castle,* Inverurie, on A96. Fifteenth-century tower house built for Leslie family. Passed by marriage to Lumsdens. Open April-September (if convenient). |

epts          Bartholomew, Lang, More.

# Lindsay

## See Crawford

Baldric de Lindsey, a Norman, is first recorded. In 1180, William de Lindsay was Baron of Luffness and Laird of Crawford. Sir David of Crawford, living about 1340, acquired Glenesk in Angus by marriage with Maria Abernethy. He had two sons, Alexander of Glenesk, father of David who was created Earl of Crawford in 1398 and married a daughter of Robert II, and Sir William of the Byres. John, 10th Lord Lindsay of Byres, a descendant of the 6th Baron of Crawford, was created Earl of Lindsay in 1366.

Sir David Lindsay of the Mount was a famous Lord Lyon King of Arms.

| PLACES of INTEREST | | |
|---|---|---|
| **FIFE** | | |
| NORTH EAST FIFE | *Balcarres,* Colinsburgh. Estate purchased in 1587. Seat of Earl of Crawford and Balcarres. No admission. | |
| | *Ceres Church,* 2½ miles SE of Cupar. Mediaeval mausoleum of Crawfords adjoins church (1806). | |
| | *Kilconquhar,* 4 miles E of Largo, seat of Earls of Lindsay. Now developed as holiday homes. | |
| **LOTHIAN** | | |
| EAST LOTHIAN | *The Byres,* by Haddington. Site of what was seat of Lindsay of the Byres. | |
| **STRATHCLYDE** | | |
| LANARK | *Tower Lindsay,* on B797, off A74, near Crawford. Fragment remains. | |
| **TAYSIDE** | | |
| ANGUS | *Edzell Castle,* Brechin, off B966. Fourteenth-century. Crawford Lindsays acquired the castle and built a new castle in the sixteenth century. Open to the public. | |
| | *Glen Esk.* Upper part of valley of River North Esk. | |

| **Septs** | Crawford, Deuchar, Lindsay. |
|---|---|

# Livingston

Leving, a Saxon, held lands in West Lothian in the twelfth century. These lands were called Leving's-toun. Members of this family were prominent in Scottish history between 1300 and 1715. They held several peerages, notably the earldoms of Callendar, Linlithgow and Newburgh.

The small Highland clan of Livingston, from the Isle of Lismore and Western Argyll, originally bore a Gaelic name spelt in differing ways — MacDunsleinhe, Mac-an-Leigh or Maclea.

There is no known blood relationship between Lowland and Highland families.

| | | |
|---|---|---|
| **PLACES NTEREST** | **CENTRAL** STIRLING | *Callendar,* Falkirk, held by Livingstons since the fourteenth century. House has fifteenth-century tower. Privately owned. *Kilsyth.* Held by Livingstons of Callendar from the early fifteenth century. Castle is now a ruin. |
| | **LOTHIAN** WEST LOTHIAN | *Livingston.* Held since the twelfth century. Almshouses founded by Henry Livingston in 1496. Lands now site of New Town. |
| | **STRATHCLYDE** ARGYLL AND BUTE | *Bachuil,* Isle of Lismore. Home of the Livingstones of Bachuil. St Moluag's Staff, amongst oldest ecclesiastical relics, held there. (Ferry from Oban or Port Appin. Telephone: Lismore 256.) |
| | LANARK | *Blantyre.* David Livingstone (1813-73), the famous explorer, was born here. There is a National Memorial, open all year round. |

# Lockhart

Originally this family came from England, and settled at Lee in Lanarkshire (1272). Sir Simon Locard carried the key to the casket in which Robert Bruce's heart was placed, and to commemorate this, the family name was changed to Lockhart. On the Crusades, he acquired the Lee Penny, the original of Sir Walter Scott's 'Talisman'.

| | | |
|---|---|---|
| **PLACES of INTEREST** | **STRATHCLYDE** | |
| | KYLE AND CARRICK | *Barr Castle,* Girvan. Fifteenth-century tower erected by the Lockharts. John Knox preached here. Privately owned. |
| | LANARK | Lands of *Carwath* held by Lockharts since the seventeenth century. |
| | | *Fatlips Castle,* Tinto Hill. Stronghold near Symington. Now a ruin. |
| | | Lands of *Lee* acquired in the twelfth century. The castle was rebuilt in the nineteenth century. |

# Logan or MacLennan

There are two distinct families: Highland and Lowland. Of the latter, Sir Robert Logan of Restalrig married a daughter of King Robert II and in 1400, he was appointed an Admiral of Scotland.

The MacLennans of the north are descended from the Logans of Drumderfit, Easter Ross. The MacLennans were anciently titled Lords of Loch Erne. In Ossianic poetry, Lide MacLennan and his clan of 1200 men appear. The MacLennans were given dependent territories in Lorne, Mull, Tiree and Iona, but after a defeat at Inverness retired to Glenshiel where they remained for centuries.

| PLACES of INTEREST | | |
|---|---|---|
| **HIGHLAND** | | |
| ROSS AND CROMARTY | *Drumderfit.* Held by the Logans before the fifteenth century. | |
| SKYE AND LOCHALSH. | *Glen Shiel.* Visitor Centre at Morvich, Shiel Bridge. National Trust for Scotland. | |
| **LOTHIAN** | | |
| BERWICKSHIRE | *Fast Castle,* NW of Coldingham, off A1107. Passed by marriage to last Logan of Restalrig in 1580. He died here after being outlawed for his involvement in the Gowrie Conspiracy. | |
| MIDLOTHIAN | *Restalrig,* Edinburgh. Lands belonged to Lestalric family; by marriage they passed to the Logans in the fourteenth century, but were confiscated after the Gowrie Conspiracy. | |

| **Septs** | Lobban |
|---|---|

113

# Lumsden

The name derived from the lands of that name on the coast of Berwickshire, near Coldingham and first mentioned in a Charter dated 1098 of Edgar, King of Scots. The earliest recorded owners of these lands are Gillen and Cren de Lumisden, who witnessed various charters in 1166, and Adam Lumsden of that Ilk who, together with Roger de Lummesdene did forced homage to Edward I of England in 1296. The family acquired lands of Blanerne, Berwickshire by Charter in 1329, and by the mid-fourteenth century offshoots had charters to Conlan in Fife and Medlar and Cushnie in Aberdeenshire.

| PLACES of INTEREST | | |
|---|---|---|
| **BORDERS** | | |
| BERWICKSHIRE | *Blanerne* or *Lumsden Castle*, Duns. No admission. Lands acquired by Charter in 1329. | |
| **FIFE** | | |
| NORTH EAST FIFE | *Airdrie*, Crail. Barony belonging to Lumsdens from 1450. Castle built in 1588. Privately owned. | |
| **GRAMPIAN** | | |
| GORDON | *Cushnie*, Alford. Seat of Head of House. Privately owned. *Pitcaple Castle*, Inverurie, beside A96. Fifteenth-century. Passed by marriage from Leslies to Lumsdens. April-September, if convenient. | |
| KINCARDINE AND DEESIDE | *Tillycairn Castle*, Cluny. Built by Lumsdens. Ruinous. Plans for restoration as clan centre and museum are in hand. | |

# MacAllister

A branch of Clan Donald which traces its origin to a great-grandson of Somerled. Clan lands were in Kintyre and the seat was on the north west side of West Loch, Tarbert. A later seat was Loup. These lands were held until the early nineteenth century. Kennox, in Ayrshire, was acquired by marriage. The clan was numerically strong in Bute and Arran.

| PLACES of INTEREST | STRATHCLYDE | |
|---|---|---|
| | ARGYLL AND BUTE | *Tarbert Castle,* Tarbert, Loch Fyne. MacAllisters were Constables. Privately owned. |
| | KILMARNOCK AND LOUDON | *Kennox,* 2½ miles W of Stewarton — late seat of clan. |

| Sept | Alexander |
|---|---|

# MacAlpine

Siol Alpine is a name which appears in a number of Clans with no apparent connection. Considered to be a Branch of the Royal Clan Alpin, Kings of Dalriada. The clan chief, however, seems to have disappeared.

| PLACES of INTEREST | STRATHCLYDE | |
|---|---|---|
| | ARGYLL AND BUTE | *Dunstaffnage Castle,* Dunstaffnage, near Oban, off A85. Capital of Dalriada. Traditional home of MacAlpines, being the site of the Scottish court. Kenneth MacAlpine became the first king of Picts and Scots and removed the Stone of Destiny and his court to Scone. Open to the public. |

| Sept | Alpin |
|---|---|

# MacArthur

One of the oldest of Argyllshire clans, claimed to be the older branch of Clan Campbell. They supported Robert Bruce and were granted extensive lands in Argyll, including those of the MacDougalls who had opposed Bruce.

| PLACES of INTEREST | STRATHCLYDE | |
|---|---|---|
| | ARGYLL AND BUTE | *Dunstaffnage Castle,* Dunstaffnage, off A85, 4 miles N of Oban. MacArthur chief was appointed Captain in the fourteenth century. |

| **Septs** | Arthur, MacArtair, MacArter. |
|---|---|

# MacAulay

There are two clans of this name. One was a branch of Clan Alpine, and in the sixteenth century entered into an agreement with the MacGregors of Glenstrae. The MacAulays of Lewis, of Norse descent and unconnected with the MacAulays of Ardencaple, were followers of the MacLeods of Lewis. The name appears in Sutherland, and in Ross-shire around Ullapool.

| PLACES of INTEREST | STRATHCLYDE | |
|---|---|---|
| | ARGYLL AND BUTE | *Ardencaple,* Gareloch. Lands retained by the MacAulays until the 12th chief sold them to Duke of Argyll in 1767. |

| Septs | Macphedran, Macphedron. |
|---|---|

# MacBean or MacBain

## See Clan Chattan

The MacBeans are believed to have come from Lochaber and settled in eastern Inverness-shire. Myles MacBean supported Mackintosh against the Red Comyn. The principal family was MacBean of Kinchyle. In 1959 an American, descended from the MacBeans of Kinchyle, was acknowledged by the Lord Lyon King of Arms as chief.

| PLACES of INTEREST | HIGHLAND INVERNESS | *Kinchyle,* south shore of Loch Ness. North of Dores, on Inverness road, road signposted to Kinchyle. Here is MacBain Memorial Park, created by Hughston MacBain of MacBain, 21st Chief. |
| --- | --- | --- |

epts      Bain, Bean, MacBain, MacBean, MacBeath, MacBeth, Macilvian, MacVean.

# MacColl

The MacColls are a branch of the Clan Donald. They settled around Loch Fyne and joined in the feud with the MacGregors.

| PLACES of INTEREST | STRATHCLYDE | |
|---|---|---|
| | ARGYLL AND BUTE | *Kenmore,* Loch Fyne. Monument to Evan McColl, 1898, Gaelic poet. |

# MacCorquodale

A distant sept of the MacLeods of Lewis. Lands held on the northern side of Loch Awe were granted to Torquil, the forebear of this family, by King Kenneth MacAlpine.

| **PLACES of INTEREST** | **STRATHCLYDE** | |
|---|---|---|
| | ARGYLL | *Loch Tromlee,* 2 miles N of Taycreggan. Ancient seat of MacCorquodales. |

# MacCulloch

Lulach was the king of Scots who succeeded MacBeth. The Highland MacCullochs seem to have owned considerabl[e] lands in the Province of Ross, and took protection from the Earls of Ross. MacCullochs in Argyllshire tended to be associated with the Clan MacDougall.

The lowland MacCullochs were prominent in Wigtownshire and Galloway.

| PLACES of INTEREST | DUMFRIES AND GALLOWAY | |
|---|---|---|
| | WIGTOWN | *Barholm Castle,* Creetown. Sixteenth seventeenth-century. MacCulloch stronghold. Now ruined. |
| | | *Cardoness Castle,* Gatehouse-of-Fleet, on A75. Fifteenth-century. MacCulloch stronghold after 1450. Open all year. |
| | | *Myreton Castle,* Port William. Originally home of MacCullochs; lands acquired by Maxwells of Monreith 1685. |

# MacDonald

The Clan Donald was indisputably the largest of all the Highland clans, controlling virtually the whole of Scotland's western seaboard from the Butt of Lewis in the north to the Mull of Kintyre in the south, with possessions in Ireland also, and in the Isle of Man. The Clan claims descent from Conn of the Hundred Battles, Ard-Righ or High-King of Ireland in the first century AD, through Colla Uais, the first of the family to settle in the Hebrides, and from whom comes the designation 'Clann Cholla', the children of Coll. Somerled, Lord of Argyll in the twelfth century, unable to overcome completely the Norse invaders, married Ragnhildis, daughter of Olave the Red of Norway. Both through marriage and later by conquest, Somerled acquired power over the Isles. After his death, his sons inherited their shares of the islands, and through them descend the MacDougalls of Argyll and Lorn, and the Clan Donald, or the MacDonalds of Islay.

The name of the Clan Donald derives from Donald of Islay, grandson of the mighty Somerled; Donald, among other children, had two sons, Angus Mor and Alasdair Mor. From the latter descend the Clan Alister (MacAlisters of Loup). Angus's son, Angus Og, supported Robert Bruce and was granted many of the vast territories formerly possessed by his ancestors. In 1354 John took the title *Dominus Insularum*. From his natural son Iain nan Fraoch descended the MacDonalds of Glencoe; his legitimate son John married his distant cousin Amy MacRuari and assumed the title Lord of the Isles. He later divorced his wife and married Margaret, daughter of King Robert II. Amy's eldest son was progenitor of the MacDonalds of Clanranald and the MacDonells of Glengarry. Princess Margaret's eldest son succeeded as Lord of the Isles; her second son, Iain Mor, 'The Tanister', founded the MacDonalds of Islay and Kintyre and, by his marriage to Marjorie Bisset of Antrim in Ireland, the MacDonnells of Antrim; the third surviving son, Alexander or Alister Carrach became Lord of Lochaber and founded the MacDonalds of Keppoch. Donald of Harlaw was succeeded by his eldest son, Alexander, who inherited, through his mother, the Earldom of Ross in 1424. He was succeeded by his son John, the fourth and last MacDonald Lord of the Isles and Earl of Ross. John's inability to govern resulted in a bloody civil war against his nephew and heir, Alexander, and his illegitimate son, Angus, in which the Lord of the Isles was defeated at the naval engagement known as the Battle of Bloody Bay, an the title was eventually forfeited in 1493. Since then the Lordship of the Isles has, with the Dukedom of Rothesay been retained by the eldest son of the reigning British monarch. It is, therefore, currently one of the titles held b HRH Prince Charles, Prince of Wales.

The decline of the MacDonald dynasty in the West Highlands runs parallel with the decline of Gaelic culture Despite attempts by several successive MacDonald leade to re-establish the old order, particularly against the rise o Campbell power, by the seventeenth century the variou branches — Sleat, Clanranald, Glengarry, Keppoch, Glencoe — had all become independent clans with their own chiefs, none of whom would claim to be Mac Dhomhnuill. This was the situation throughout the troublesome times of the seventeenth century and the Jacobite risings of the eighteenth century until the Battle Culloden in 1746 and the end of the Clan system. Not un 1947 was Clan Donald again to have a High Chief, when th Lord Lyon King of Arms granted the 7th Lord MacDona the undifferenced Arms of MacDonald of Macdonald, Chief of the Name and Arms.

| | | |
|---|---|---|
| **PLACES of INTEREST** | **HIGHLAND** LOCHABER | *Castle Tioram*, Moidart. N of A861. Ruined stronghold of the MacDonald of Clanranald. *Glenfinnan*. Monument raised by MacDonald of Glenaladale to the me who fought for the Prince in 1745-4 *Invergarry Castle*, Invergarry. Ruine stronghold of the MacDonells of Glengarry. Well of the Heads, wher heads of the murderers of Keppoch said to have been washed by Iain Lom Bard of Keppoch. |

| SKYE AND LOCHALSH | *Isle of Skye:* The Clan Donald Centre, Armadale Castle, Armadale, Sleat. Various ruined Castles and Flora MacDonald's grave. |
|---|---|

## STRATHCLYDE

| ARGYLL AND BUTE | *Finlaggan,* Isle of Islay. Ruins of palatial residence of the Lords of the Isles. *Dunnyvaig Castle* — ruined seat of the MacDonalds of Islay and Kintyre. *Glencoe.* Memorial to those who perished in the Massacre of 1692. Glencoe and North Lorn Folk Museum — MacIan's bible and drinking cup and other items of clan interest. |
|---|---|

## LOTHIAN

| EDINBURGH | *Scottish National Portrait Gallery,* Edinburgh. Raeburn's portrait of MacDonell of Glengarry. *National Museum of Antiquities of Scotland* — portraits of Sleat MacDonald boys, first Lord MacDonald and General Sir James MacDonell. *Royal Scottish Museum* — Broadsword and targe of Alexander MacDonald of Keppoch. |
|---|---|

**Septs**  Alaister, Alcock, Alexander, Alison, Allan, Allanson, Allen, Allister, Anderson, Ballach, Balloch, Beath, Beaton, Bethune, Bowie, Brodie, Budge, Buie, Bulloch, Callan, Callen, Cambridge, Cathal, Cathil, Cochran, Cochrane, Coll, Colson, Conn, Connal, Connell, Cook, Cooke, Coull, Coulson, Cowan, Cririe, Cromb, Crombie, Croom, Crum, Currie, Daniel, Daniels, Darrach, Darroch, Donald, Donaldson, Donnell, Donnelson, Donnilson, Drain, Dunnel, Forrest, Forrester, Galbraith, Galbreath, Gall, Galt, Gaul, Gauld, Gault, Gilbridge, Gill, Gorrie, Gorry, Gowan, Gowans, Hawthorn, Henderson, Hendrie, Hendry, Henry, Heron, Hewison, Houston, Houstoun, Howat, Howe, Howie, Howison, Hudson, Hughson, Hutcheon, Hutcheson, Hutchin, Hutchinson, Hutchison, Hutchon, Hutson, Isaac, Isaacs, Isles, Jeffrey, Johnson, Johnstone, Kean, Keegan, Keene, Keighren, Kelly, Ketchen, Ketchin, Kinnell, Laing, Lang, Leitch, MacAchin, MacAichan, MacAllan, MacArthur, MacBeath, MacBheath, MacBrayne, MacBride, MacBryde, MacBurie, MacCaa, MacCairn, MacCambridge, MacCarron, MacCaw, MacCay, MacCluskie, MacCodrum, MacColl, MacConnal, MacConnell, MacCooish, MacCook, MacCosham, MacCowan, MacCrain, MacCran, MacCrindle, MacCrire, MacCrorie,

MacCrum, MacCuig, MacCuish, MacCuithein, MacCurrach, MacCurie, MacCutchen, MacCutcheon, MacDaniell, MacDonald, MacDonnell, MacDrain, MacEachan, MacEachen, MacEachern, MacEachin, MacEachran, MacElfrish, MacElheran, MacGaa, MacGachan, MacGaw, MacGeachan, MacGeachy, MacGechie, MacGee, MacGhee, MacGhie, MacGill, MacGillivantic, MacGilp, MacGlasrich, MacGorrie, MacGorry, MacGoun, MacGow, MacGowan, MacGown, MacGrain, MacHendrie, MacHendry, MacHenry, MacHugh, MacHutchen, MacHutcheon, MacIan, MacIllrick, MacIlreach, MacIlrevie, MacIlriach, MacIlwraith, MacIlwrick, MacIsaac, MacKain, MacKane, MacKay, MacKeachan, MacKeachie, MacKean, MacKeand, MacKechnie, MacKee, MacKellaig, MacKelloch, MacKeochan, MacKerron, MacKessack, Mackessick, MacKey, MacKichan, MacKie, MacKiggan, MacKillop, MacKinnell, MacKistock, MacLairish, MacLardy, MacLarty, MacLaverty, MacLeverty, MacMichie, MacMurchie, MacMurchy, MacMurdo, MacMurdoch, MacMurray, MacMukrich, MacOwan, Mac O'Shannaig, MacPhilip, MacQuilkan, MacQuistan, MacQuisten, MacRaith, MacRearie, MacRonald, MacRorie, MacRory, MacRuer, MacRury, MacRyrie, MacSorlet, MacSporran, MacSwan, MacSween, MacVarish, MacVurich, MacVurie, MacVurrich, MacWhan, MacWhannell, Mark, Marquis, Martin, May, Mechie, Meekison, Mekie, Michael, Michie, Michieson, Murchie, Murchison, Murdoch, Murdochson, Murphy, O'May, Park, Paton, Patten, Peden, Philip, Philipson, Phillip, Phillips, Philp, Purcell, Rainnie, Rennie, Reoch, Revie, Riach, Roderick, Ronald, Ronaldson, Rorie, Rorison, Ryrie, Sander, Sanders, Sanderson, Saunders, Shannon, Shennan, Sorley, Sorlie, Sporran, Train, Whannel, Whellan, Wheelan, Wilkie, Wilkinson

# MacDougall

Dougal or Dugald, son of Somerled, originated this Clan. MacDougall of Lorn was on the losing side in the contest between Bruce and the Comyns, and was deprived of his lands. They were restored on a MacDougall marriage to Robert Bruce's granddaughter. The chiefship, therefore, was held by MacDougall of Dunollie.

| **PLACES of INTEREST** | **STRATHCLYDE** | |
| --- | --- | --- |
| | ARGYLL AND BUTE | *Ardchattan Priory,* Loch Etive. Valliscaulian house founded by MacDougalls in 1231. Open all times. |
| | | *Gylen Castle,* Kerrera. Fortress of the MacDougall Lords of Lorn. Possibly thirteenth-century, now roofless. Passenger ferry from Oban. |
| | | *Dunollie Castle,* Oban. Twelfth-century stronghold of the MacDougalls of Lorn. The 'Brooch of Lorn' once owned by Robert Bruce is held at Dunollie House, below castle. No admission. |
| | | *Dunstaffnage,* N of Oban, off A85. Once the fortified seat of the Kings of Dalriada; the castle is thirteenth-century. It passed from the MacDougalls of Lorn to the Campbells. |

**Septs**

Carmichael, Conacher, Cowan, Dougall, Livingston, MacConacher, MacCowan, MacCulloch, MacDowall, MacGoughan, MacKichan, MacLugash, MacLukas, MacLulich, MacNemell.

# MacDuff

MacDuff, 1st Earl of Fife, was held to be the Earl of Fife who killed MacBeth. The MacDuffs held the privilege of crowning the king.

The old earldom became extinct in 1353 on the death of Duncan, the 12th Earl. William Duff, Lord Braco, was created Earl of Fife in 1759 in the Irish peerage. In 1827, James, 4th Earl was raised to the peerage of Great Britain, and Alexander, 6th of this line was made Duke of Fife in 1889 when he married Queen Victoria's granddaughter, Princess Louise.

| PLACES of INTEREST | | |
|---|---|---|
| **FIFE** KIRKCALDY | | *Earlsferry* or *Elie*. Stems from the tradition that MacDuff was ferried across the Firth of Forth to Dunbar from this point when fleeing from MacBeth. |
| NORTH EAST FIFE | | *Cross of MacDuff*, Newburgh (between Perth and Cupar). According to tradition, sanctuary could be claimed here by kinsmen of the MacDuffs. |
| **GRAMPIAN** BANFF AND BUCHAN | | *Duff House*, Banff. Built by William Adam. Former seat of Earl of Fife. Open April–September. *Dufftown*. Founded 1817 by James Duff, 4th Earl of Fife. *Macduff*, on Moray Firth. Burgh of Barony for Earl of Fife, 1783. |

# MacEwen

Ewen of Otter lived in the thirteenth century. Swene, last of Otter, granted the lands of Otter to Duncan Campbell in 1432 and resigned the barony of Otter to James I, from whence it passed to the Campbells.

A large number of MacEwans settled in the Lennox, Lochaber and Galloway. Elspeth MacEwan was last witch to be put to death, in Kirkcudbright in 1698.

| **PLACES of INTEREST** | **STRATHCLYDE** | |
|---|---|---|
| | ARGYLL | *Otter Ferry,* across Loch Fyne from Lochgilphead. Lands held by MacEwens. |

# MacFarlane

Parlan or Bartholomew who lived in the reign of King David Bruce in territories at the head of Loch Lomond is said to have given his name to this clan. The MacFarlanes were considered a troublesome clan, and through Acts of Estates were deprived of their lands and scattered in the seventeenth century.

| PLACES of INTEREST | STRATHCLYDE | |
|---|---|---|
| | ARGYLL AND BUTE | *Arrochar* at the head of Loch Long. Lands acquired by 6th Chief from the Earl of Lennox. *Tarbet,* on Loch Lomond. Eilean-a-Vow — islet on which stands ruined Inveruglas Castle, twice besieged by Cromwell. *'Loch Sloy'* was the war cry taken from a small loch under Ben Vorlich. Now part of Hydro-Electric scheme. |

**Septs**

Allan, Allenson, Bartholomew, Caw, Galbraith, Lennox, MacCondy, MacJames, Mackinlay, Maclooch, MacNair, MacNides, MacNiter, MacWalter MacWilliam, Monach, Napier, Parlane, Robb, Stalker, Thomason, Weaver, Weir.

# MacFie, MacDuffie or MacPhee

A branch of Clan Alpin. MacDuffie of Colonsay was reported to be hereditary keeper of the records for the Lords of the Isles. The MacFies held Colonsay until the mid-seventeeth century when they scattered. Some followed Lochiel, others the Islay MacDonalds.

| PLACES of INTEREST | STRATHCLYDE | |
|---|---|---|
| | ARGYLL AND BUTE | Colonsay. 8 mile-long island. Boat from Oban 3 days a week. |

epts     Duffy, Duffie, MacGuffie, Mackaffie.

# MacGillivray

### See Clan Chattan

Originally from Morvern and Lochaber, they took
protection from Mackintosh in the thirteenth century. I
1500 they settled in Strathnairn in Inverness-shire.
Alexander, chief of Clan, led the Clan Chattan Regiment a
Culloden.

| PLACES of INTEREST | HIGHLAND INVERNESS | |
|---|---|---|
| | | *Dunlichty Churchyard,* Strathnairn, 6 miles from Daviot. Burial ground o MacGillivrays. |
| | | *Dunmaglass,* Strathnairn. MacGilliv-rays settled here in 1500. |

| Septs | Gilroy, MacGillivoor, MacGilroy, MacGilvra, MacGilvray, MacGilvrae, MacIlroy. |
|---|---|

# MacGregor

Senior Clan of the Clan Alpin, said to be descendants of Griogar, third son of Kenneth MacAlpine, King of Scots in the ninth century. At one time they held lands in Perthshire and Argyllshire — Glenstrae, Glenlochy, Glenlyon and Glengyle. They were relieved of these by the powerful Clan Campbell, resorted to violence and became raiders and killers.

In 1603 the Clan Gregor won a victory at Glen Fruin over the Colquhouns, who held the Royal Commission; it was the ultimate act of rebellion, and the crown therefore decided to outlaw the clan. Those who were not hunted down and exterminated were forced to change their name.

When Montrose raised Charles I's standard in 1644, the Laird of MacGregor joined him; but the clan was not restored finally to their rightful name until 1775.

| PLACES of INTEREST | CENTRAL STIRLING | *Inversnaid*, Loch Lomond. A path leads N to Rob Roy's cave. Robert Bruce is said to have hidden here in 1306. |
|---|---|---|
| Places of Interest | STRATHCLYDE ARGYLL AND BUTE | *Balquhidder.* The outlaw Rob Roy MacGregor (1671-1734) had Balquhidder farm here. Balquhidder Church has the grave of Rob Roy. *Glenorchy* — bestowed on MacGregors for services rendered to Alexander II. |
| | DUMBARTON | *Glen Fruin,* 1603. 200 Colquhouns and onlookers were killed by the MacGregors, who were later outlawed for the deed by King James VI. *Inchcailloch,* off Balmaha. Burial place of the Macgregors. |

Septs

Black, Caird, Comrie, Dochart, Fletcher, Gregor, Gregorson, Gregory, Greig, Grewar, Grier, Gruer, Grigor, Lechy, Leckie, Lecky, MacAdam, Macara, Macaree, MacChoiter, MacConachie, MacGrouther, MacGruder, MacGruther, MacGruitte, Macilduy, MacLeister, MacLiver, MacNee, MacNeish, MacNie, MacNish, MacPeter, MacPetrie, Malloch, Neish, Nish, Peter, White, Whyte.

# MacInnes

Originates from the Dalriads. A family of MacInneses were hereditary bowmen to the chief of Clan Mackinnon.

| PLACES of INTEREST the | STRATHCLYDE | |
|---|---|---|
| | ARGYLL AND BUTE | *Kinlochaline Castle,* Morvern. Fifteenth-century castle. A chief of the MacInneses was Keeper in the seventeenth century. |

**Septs**     Angus, MacAngus, MacCainsh, MacCansh, MacMaster.

# MacIntyre

### See Clan Chattan

The 'Children of the Carpenter' who came from the Hebrides and settled in Lorn in the fourteenth century. They are recorded as having been Hereditary Foresters to the Stewarts of Lorn. The Macintyres in Badenoch took protection from the Clan Chattan.

| **PLACES of INTEREST** | **STRATHCLYDE** | |
|---|---|---|
| | ARGYLL AND BUTE | *Glen Noe* on Loch Etive. Lands possessed for several centuries until 1806. |
| | CUMNOCK AND DOON VALLEY | *Sorn Castle,* Sorn, 3½ miles E of Mauchline. Seat of Chief; privately owned. |
| **Septs** | Tyre, MacTear, Wright. | |

# MacIver

Clan Iver Glassary is believed to have formed part of the army of King Alexander II which conquered Argyll in 1221. They came from the Glenlyon district, and in Argyll possessed Glassary and Cowal. They took protection from the Campbells.

| PLACES of INTEREST | STRATHCLYDE | |
|---|---|---|
| | ARGYLL AND BUTE | *Glassary*, containing Lochgilphead. Original location of the clan. |

# Mackay

Descent is claimed from the Royal House of Moray through the line of Morgund of Pluscarden. The clansmen were removed to Ross in 1160 by Malcolm IV and dispersed to Sutherland, where they at one time owned lands 'from Drimholisten to Kylescue'. Other Mackays lived in Galloway and Kintyre.

In 1427 the clan could muster 4000 men, which gives some idea of the strong position they acquired. Their fortunes fluctuated, however, and a period of vassalage to Huntly and to Sutherland preceded 1628, when Sir Donald Mackay of Strathnaver was made 1st Lord Reay.

'Mackay's Society' was formed in Glasgow in the early nineteenth century.

| PLACES of INTEREST | HIGHLAND SUTHERLAND | |
|---|---|---|

**PLACES of INTEREST**

**HIGHLAND**
**SUTHERLAND**

*Eddrachillis.* Held by Mackays from 1515–1757.

*Dornoch.* Clan feud between Murrays of Dornoch and the Mackays of Strathnaver led to the town being burned and plundered in 1570.

*Scourie.* Estate owned by cadet branch.

*Strathnaver.* Valley inhabited by Mackays, but sold in the seventeenth century to the Sutherlands and depopulated during the Clearances.

*Strathnaver Museum,* at Farr, near Bettyhill. Local history museum in former church, at heart of Mackay country. Open during season, Monday, Wednesday and Saturday.

*Tongue House,* Kyle of Tongue, (seventeenth-eighteenth century) was the seat of Lord Reay, but was sold to the Dukes of Sutherland.

*Tuiteam-Tarbhach* ('fertile plain of slaughter') near Inveran, 1½ miles NW of Invershin. Decisive Mackay victory over the Macleods of Assynt and Lewis.

**Septs**  Bain, Bayn, MacCie, MacCoy, MacKee, Mackie, MacPhail, MacQuey, MacQuoid, MacVail, Neilson, Paul, Polson, Williamson.

# Mackenzie

Clan Mackenzie territory was probably much of Mid–Ross and round Muir of Ord, but in the twelfth century they were removed to Wester Ross (Kintail) by William the Lion. They were joined by the MacRaes, who became their Chief's bodyguard, and the MacLennans, who became their hereditary standard bearers.

In 1263, the Battle of Largs terminated the power of the Vikings in the West, and the MacKenzies were given the right to be part of the Royal Bodyguard, an honour they kept up to the Battle of Flodden. Colin MacKenzie, for his services to Kings Alexander II and III was given Royal Charter for the lands of Kintail.

Alexander 'Ionraech', 7th Chief of Kintail, is recorded in the fifteenth century. His grandson, John, fought at Flodden, and John's grandson, Colin, fought for Queen Mary at Langside. Colin's eldest son, Kenneth, became Lord Mackenzie of Kintail in 1609, and his descendants number the MacKenzies of Pluscarden and Lochslinn. His eldest son was made Earl of Seaforth in 1623. When he died without issue, the title passed to his half–brother who went to Holland after the execution of Charles I and was later Secretary of State for Scotland. Another of Colin's sons, Sir Ruaridh MacKenzie of Castle Leod, Coigach and Tarbat, was ancestor of the Earls of Cromartie.

The Earl of Cromartie was condemned to death after the '45, but was reprieved. For a generation, the Cromartie Estates were confiscated, and the Earl's son who had fled abroad eventually became a Lieutenant–General in Sweden. King George III allowed him back in 1777 and he raised the 71st Highlanders whom he took to India. This Regiment became the H.L.I. and was raised before the Seaforth Highlanders (1778). The main Seaforth line died out in 1815. Tenants of the Seaforth estates were evicted by the Trustees, but they were taken in by the Cromartie Mackenzies. The Lord Lyon King of Arms has recognised the Earl of Cromartie as Chief of the Clan Mackenzie.

| PLACES of INTEREST | HIGHLAND ROSS AND CROMARTY | *Castle Leod,* Strathpeffer. Home of the Earl of Cromartie. Viewed by appointment. |
| --- | --- | --- |

*Chanonry Point, Black Isle.* Memorial to the Brahan Seer who supposedly prophesied the end of the Seaforth line. The prophecy was made two generations before the Seaforth Earldom was created, and despite the surprising accuracy of the prophecies attributed to this 'Coineach Odhar' the stories are believed to have originated from a number of sources.

*Fortrose.* Portraits of Seaforth Mackenzies in the Town Hall.

**SKYE AND LOCHALSH**

*Eilean Donan.* Castle and famous beauty spot, headquarters of the clan in the twelfth century.

Eilean Donan Castle

**STRATHCLYDE**

ARGYLL AND BUTE

*Island of Iona.* Early chiefs buried here.

epts

Charlson, Kenneth, Kennethson, MacConnach, MacIver, MacIvor, MacKerlich, MacMurchie, MacVanich, MacVinish, Murchie, Murchison, MacThearlaich.

# Mackinlay

The clan country of the Mackinlays was the Lennox District, but records are vague. The Mackinlays of Lennox descended from Findlay, a son of Buchanan of Drumikill. Like other Lennox clans, many Mackinlays emigrated to the USA. Mackinlays were also connected with the Clan Farquharson, descendants of Farquharson of Braemar in the sixteenth century. There were Findlays or Mackinlays also in Lochalsh and Kintail. Variant spellings of Mackinlay are Donleavy, Finlay, Findlay, Finlayson, Macinally, Mackinley.

# Mackinnon

A branch of Clan Alpin from Fingon, great grandson of King Kenneth MacAlpin.

The Mackinnons were vassals of the Lords of the Isles and were at times 'master of the household' and 'marshal of the army' for the Lords of the Isles. For many generations a branch held the post of hereditary Standard Bearer to the MacDonalds of Sleat. Lands were on Mull and Strathordell in the Isle of Skye.

| PLACES of INTEREST | | |
|---|---|---|
| | **HIGHLAND** | |
| | SKYE AND LOCHALSH | *Dunakin* (Castle Maoil), Isle of Skye, Kyle Akin. Twelfth-fifteenth century, once a Mackinnon stronghold. |
| | **STRATHCLYDE** | |
| | ARGYLL AND BUTE | *Mackinnon's Cave,* Ardmeanach Peninsula, Isle of Mull. Only accessible at low tide. The name was taken from piper who undertook to lead a party through the cave, but who disappeared. His dog reappeared, hairless with fright, on the clifftop some distance away. This story is found relating to various other caves on the west coast of Scotland. |

epts        Love, Mackinney, Mackinny, Mackinven, MacMorran.

# Mackintosh

### See Clan Chattan

The name Mackintosh means the 'son of the thane'. Traditionally the founder is said to have been a son of MacDuff, ancestor of the Earls of Fife. The Mackintoshes were later connected with the Chiefship of Clan Chattan, when Angus, 6th Chief, married Eva, heiress of Clan Chattan, in 1291. Lands in Glenloy and Locharkaig in Lochaber followed, sparking off major feuds with the Earls of Moray and Huntly, and with the Camerons, and Gordons. The later additions of Glenroy and Glenspean led to trouble with the MacDonnells of Keppoch.

The clan feuds were not settled until the late seventeenth century, when Mackintosh gained control of Glenroy and Glenspean, Cameron of Lochiel, the superiority of Glenloy and Locharkaig.

The Mackintosh line dwindled and the senior lines died out; but interest and clanship has been revived in recent years.

| PLACES of INTEREST | HIGHLAND | |
|---|---|---|
| | INVERNESS | *Moy,* Inverness. Seat of Chief. No admission. |
| | | *Petty Parish Church,* on edge of Moray Firth. Burial place of the Mackintosh chiefs. |
| | LOCHABER | *Mulroy,* near Roy Bridge, Keppoch. The last clan battle in Scotland is said to have taken place here between the Mackintoshes and Clan Ranald. |

**Septs**

Adamson, Ayson, Aysons of NZ, Clark, Clarke, Clarkson, Clerk, Crerar, Dallas, Elder, Esson, Glen, Glennie, Gollan, Hardie, Hardy, Heggie, MacAndrew, MacAy, MacCardney, MacClerie, MacClerish, MacChlery, MacConely, MacGlashen, Machardie, Machardy, MacKeggie, Mackey, McKillieren, MacNiven, MacRitchie, Niven, Noble, Paul, Ritchie, Seath, Seth, Shaw, Tarrill, Tosh, Toshech.

# MacLachlan

The original seat of the Clan MacLachlan would appear to be Lochaber and through marriage they acquired lands in Cowal. Gillespie MacLachlan attended the first Parliament of Robert Bruce in 1309. The clan territory is now reduced to a strip on the eastern side of Loch Fyne.

| PLACES of INTEREST | STRATHCLYDE |  |
|---|---|---|
| | ARGYLL AND BUTE | *Castle Lachlan,* Loch Fyne. Twelfth-thirteenth-century and early sixteenth-century. The tower was destroyed after Culloden. Now ruined. (For key, apply Inver Cottage Tea Room.) *Inchconnel Castle,* Loch Awe. A cadet branch of the MacLachlans were captains of Inchonnel from 1613. |

**Septs**

Ewan, Ewen, Ewing, Gilchrist, Lachlan, MacEwan, MacEwen, MacGilchrist, Mauchlan.

# MacLaine of Lochbuie

## See Maclean

Descended from Eachin Reganach, brother of Lachlan Lubanach, who was the forebear of the MacLeans of Duart. The brothers lived during the reign of Robert II. The chiefship was settled by tanistry and Duart is recognised as chief of Clan Maclean, although Eachin Reganach was, in fact, an elder brother of Lachlan Lubanach. Charles, son of Eachin was progenitor of the Macleans of Glen Urquhart and Dochgarroch, a sept of Clan Chattan.

The Maclaines were followers of the Lord of the Isles, and were granted lands in Mull.

| **PLACES of INTEREST** | **STRATHCLYDE** | |
|---|---|---|
| | ARGYLL AND BUTE | *Castle Moy,* Loch Buie, Isle of Mull. Ruined keep which, for over 500 years, was the home of the MacLaines of Lochbuie. |

| **Septs** | MacCormick, MacFadyen, MacFadzean, MacGilvra, MacIlvora, MacPhadden, Patten. |
|---|---|

# Maclaren
## Clan Labhran

There are two races of Maclaren, one in Perthshire, and the Maclaurins, said at one time to have owned the Isle of Tiree. The native clan lands of the former are in Strathearn and Balquhidder. The Maclaren chiefs were Hereditary Celtic Abbots of Achtow in Balquhidder. The Clan was active in the Jacobite cause in the Risings of 1715 and 1745, and fought at Culloden. By the eighteenth century, the clan was largely dispersed — many clansmen to Canada.

| PLACES of INTEREST | TAYSIDE PERTH AND KINROSS | *Achleskine,* near foot of Loch Voil. Remained in family of chief until 1892. *Balquhidder,* at E end of Loch Voil. Ruins of thirteenth-century church. |
|---|---|---|

| Septs | MacGrory, MacPatrick, MacRoy, Paterson. |
|---|---|

# Maclean

### See also MacLaine of Lochbuie

Descendants of Gillean of the Battleaxe, they were removed from Moray by Malcolm IV. Lachlan Lubanach, brother of Eachin Reganach who founded the MacLaines of Lochbuie, was the progenitor of this clan. They settled in Lorn and through service to the Lords of the Isles were awarded lands on Mull. In 1493, when the last Lord of the Isles was forfeited, the Macleans held extensive estates on Mull, Tiree, Islay and Jura, in Morvern, Lochaber and Knapdale. Lands were divided among four branches: the Macleans of Duart, Macleans of Ardgour, Macleans of Coll and the MacLaines of Lochbuie.

| PLACES of INTEREST | STRATHCLYDE | |
|---|---|---|
| | ARGYLL AND BUTE | *Ardgour;* district between Loch Linnhe, Morvern and Loch Shiel. Held by Macleans of Ardgour. |
| | | *Breachacha Castle,* Isle of Coll. Fifteenth–century stronghold held alternately by Macleans of Coll and of Duart. |
| | | *Duart Castle,* Duart Bay, Isle of Mull. Fourteenth–century but dates from 1250. Seat of Macleans of Duart. Burned by Argyll in 1691. Open May–September. |

Duart Castle

**Septs**    Beath, Beaton, Black, Clanachan, Garvie, Gillan, Gillon, Gilzean, Lean, MacBeath, MacBeth, MacIlday, MacLenag, MacRankin, MacVeag, MacVey, Rankin.

# MacLeod

This clan descends from Leod, son of Olaf (the Black), King of the Isle of Man. He was fostered to Paul Balkasson, Sheriff of Skye and about 1220 married the daughter and heiress of MacRaild.

Leod had four sons — the eldest, Tormod (Norman), inherited Dunvegan and Harris, becoming chief of these lands, and adopting the title MacLeod of Dunvegan. The second, Torquil, inherited Lewis. The latter eventually failed in the male line and is now represented by the MacLeods of Raasay.

The MacLeods served under the Lords of the Isles, holding a high rank.

Throughout their history, the MacLeods have had many outstanding chiefs. In more recent years, Dame Flora MacLeod of MacLeod, who died in 1977 aged 98, did much to publicise the clan by visiting clansfolk all over the world, helping to found clan societies in Canada, Australia, New Zealand and the USA.

| PLACES of INTEREST | FIFE | |
|---|---|---|
| | NORTH EAST FIFE | *St Andrews.* In the burial ground of St Andrews Cathedral, against the west wall, is to be found the tomb of the 22nd Chief. |
| | **HIGHLAND** | |
| | SKYE AND LOCHALSH | *Boreraig,* near Dunvegan Head. Site of the MacCrimmon Cairn. *Brochel Castle,* Isle of Raasay, E Shore. Ruined home of MacLeods of Raasay. *Dunvegan Castle,* Isle of Skye. Home of the Chief. Open daily during summer months. *Kilmuir Churchyard,* 1 mile SE of Dunvegan. Burial place of the last five chiefs of MacLeod. |
| | | Other buildings of MacLeod interest in Skye such as Gesto House are now in ruins. |
| | SUTHERLAND | *Ardvreck Castle,* Assynt, A837. Built in 1591 by MacLeod of Assynt. Montrose was betrayed here. Ruins only. |

147

| | |
|---|---|
| WESTERN ISLES | *Eye Church,* Isle of Lewis. The burial place of the MacLeods of Lewis. *Lews Castle,* Stornoway. Stronghold of the MacLeods of Lewis, now demolished. Part of the grounds now contain Lews Castle Technical College. *Rodel Church and Burial Ground,* Harris. Built by Alasdair *crotach* (hump-backed). The 8th and 9th chiefs of Dunvegan are buried here. |

**LOTHIAN**

| | |
|---|---|
| EDINBURGH | *Scottish National Portrait Gallery.* Portraits, photographs and relics of MacLeod interest. *St Cuthbert's Church.* Tomb of 23rd Chief (immediately facing the apse of the church). *The White House,* Whitehouse Loan, eighteenth-century home of 22nd Chief when in Edinburgh. |

**STRATHCLYDE**

| | |
|---|---|
| ARGYLL AND BUTE | *Iona.* Where Leod and the following six chiefs are buried. |

---

**Septs**      Beaton, Caskie, Grimmond, Lewis, MacAulay, MacCaig, MacCallum, MacCrimmon, MacLure, Nicol, Nicolson, Norman, Tolmie.

---

# Macmillan

A tribe of Moray who derived from the ancient tribe of Kanteai, one of the subsidiaries of the Northern Picts. They held lands on Tayside, and Malcolm Mór Macmillan was established in Knapdale with a Charter from the Lord of the Isles by 1360. Most of these lands, however, appear to have been lost by the close of the fifteenth century. The Macmillans spread from Knapdale south into Kintyre, and to Galloway and Kirkcudbright.

A blacksmith from Dumfries-shire called Kirkpatrick Macmillan invented the pedal bicycle. Harold Macmillan, former Prime Minister of Great Britain, is descended from Malcolm MacMillan, a crofter on Arran in the eighteenth century.

| PLACES of INTEREST | | |
|---|---|---|
| **DUMFRIES AND GALLOWAY** | | |
| NITHSDALE | | *Keir,* Sanquhar. Birthplace of Kirkpatrick Macmillan who built the first pedal bicycle. He rode it to Glasgow and was fined for knocking over a pedestrian. |
| **STRATHCLYDE** | | |
| ARGYLL AND BUTE | | *Kilmory,* Knapdale, between Loch Sween and Loch Killisport. Chapel with fourteenth- or fifteenth-century Macmillan's Cross. |

Septs — Baxter, Bell, Brown, MacBaxter.

# MacNab

This clan originated with the Hereditary Celtic Abbot of Glendochart in the reign of David I. Early lands were on the shores of Loch Tay, in Strathfillan and Glen Dochart. The family emigrated to Canada in 1823, and settled in MacNab near Ottawa; some later returned.

| PLACES of INTEREST | TAYSIDE PERTH AND KINROSS | |
|---|---|---|
| | | *Eilean Ran,* on north bank of River Lochay. Site of Macnab stronghold, burnt by Cromwell's troops. *Falls of Dochart.* Islets here were MacNab burial grounds. *Glendochart.* Lands of Celtic monastery. The abbots are believed to be forebears. *Kinnell House,* Killin. Seat of Chief. |

**Septs**     Abbot, Abbotson, Dewar, Gilfillan, Macandeoir.

# MacNaughton

In the thirteenth century this clan was found in Lochawe, Glenaray, Glenshira, and Loch Fyne. Gillechrist MacNachdan was granted the keeping of the Castle of Frechelen (Fraoch Eilean) by Alexander III in 1267. In the fourteenth century Dundarave became the clan stronghold. The last MacNaughton of Dundarave was married under alcoholic influence to the wrong daughter of Sir James Campbell of Ardkinglas in 1700. On discovering the mistake the following morning, he fled with the second daughter leaving his wife pregnant. Consequently, Ardkinglas acquired MacNaughton's lands.

**PLACES of INTEREST**

**STRATHCLYDE**

ARGYLL AND BUTE

*Dundarave Castle,* Loch Fyne. Ancient MacNaughton stronghold. Building mainly sixteenth-century. Restored by Sir Robert Lorimer.
*Innis Fraoch,* Loch Awe. Castle of Fraoch Eilean. Ruined clan stronghold.

**Septs**

Hendry, Kendrick, MacBrayne, Maceol, MacHendry, Mackendrick, Mackenrick, MacKnight, MacNair, MacNayer, MacNiven, MacVicar, Niven, Weir.

# MacNeil

The clan claims to descend directly from Niall of the Nine Hostages, High King of Ireland, who came to Barra in 1049. Gilleonan Roderick Murchaid MacNeil received a Charter for the island from Alexander, Lord of the Isles in 1427. A branch of the clan acquired Colonsay and Oronsay from the Campbells. Barra was sold in 1838, and the estate bought back and Kisimul restored by Robert Lister Macneil of Barra, the immediate past Chief.

| PLACES of INTEREST | | |
|---|---|---|
| | **WESTERN ISLES** | |
| | SOUTH UIST | *Kisimul Castle,* Barra. Thirteenth-century. The tower probably dates from 1120, but most of the existing building is fifteenth-century. The ruins were restored by the current chief. Open May–September, Wednesday and Saturday p.m. Charge for boatman. |
| | | *Stack Island,* S of Isle of Eriskay. Lair of Macneil pirates. |
| | **STRATHCLYDE** | |
| | ARGYLL AND BUTE | *Castle Sween,* Knapdale. Twelfth-century Norman keep. Hereditary Keepers were the MacNeills of Gigha. |

**Septs**   Neal, Neil, Neill, MacNeilage, MacNeiledge, MacNelly.

# MacPhail

## See Clan Chattan

MacPhails traditionally came from Lochaber in early fourteenth century. They are on record with Mackintoshes in 1481. Inverernie was in the family from mid sixteenth century until it was sold about 1763.

| PLACES of INTEREST | HIGHLAND INVERNESS | |
|---|---|---|
| | | *Inverernie,* 7 miles S of Inverness on River Nairn. Privately owned. |

**Septs**   Fail, Fall, MacFail, MacFaul, MacPaul, MacPhal, MacPhaul.

# Macpherson

### See Clan Chattan

The Clan Macpherson derives its name from Duncan, Parson of Kingussie in the fifteenth century, himself a descendant of Muriach, Chief of Clan Chattan in 1173. Three brothers, Kenneth, John and Gillies, who lived in the mid–fourteenth century are believed to be the forebears of the Macphersons of Cluny, Pitmain and Invereshie respectively. In the Rising of 1745 Cluny Macpherson transferred his loyalties to the Jacobites, and for nine years following the disaster of Culloden, dodged the Government troops who sought him. The Cluny estate, restored in 1784, eventually comprised most of Laggan, and although lost during the Second World War, several acres have been settled in perpetuity as a Clan rallying ground.

| **PLACES of INTEREST** | **HIGHLAND BADENOCH AND STRATHSPEY** | *Balavil,* Kingussie. Built by James Macpherson, so–called 'translator' of fabled Ossian poems. No admission. *Newtonmore.* Clan Macpherson Museum, on old A9/A86. Clan Macpherson Rally and the Newtonmore Highland Games are held on the first Saturday in August. Gathering ground 3 miles S of Newtonmore at Craig Dubh, by Laggan Bridge. |
| --- | --- | --- |

**Septs**

Cattanach, Clark, Clarke, Clarkson, Clerk, Currie, Ferson, Gillespie, Gillies, Gow, Keith, Lees, MacChlerick, MacChlery, MacCurrack, MacGowan, MacKeith, MacLeish, Maclerie, Maclise, MacMurdo, MacMurdoch, MacMurrich, MacVurrie, Murdoch, Murdoson.

# Macquarrie

A branch of Clan Alpin who had territory on Mull and Ulva. Followers of the Lords of the Isles. Most of the family papers burned in a fire in 1688. Ulva was sold for financial reasons in 1777.

| **PLACES of INTEREST** | **STRATHCLYDE** |
|---|---|
| | ARGYLL AND BUTE |

*Gruline House,* Salen, Isle of Mull. Was the home of Major-General Lachlan Macquarie (1761–1824), first Governor of New South Wales (1810–21). Mausoleum.

*Island of Staffa.* Once comprised part of MacQuarrie estate.

*Island of Ulva.* Main MacQuarrie estates.

# MacQueen
## See Clan Chattan

Descended from 'Conn of the hundred battles', as are the MacDonalds. The Macqueens of Garafad held lands in Skye for many centuries, and the clan always maintained a close connection with Clan Donald. Eventually they became connected with Clan Chattan Federation through the marriage of Mora MacDonald of Moidart to the 10th Chief of Mackintosh, and were known as Clan Revan, from a kinsman of the bride, Revan MacMulmor MacAngus Macqueen.

| **PLACES of INTEREST** | **HIGHLAND** INVERNESS | *Corrybrough,* estate 1 mile E of Tomatin. Lands belonged to Clan Revan from the fifteenth–eighteenth centuries. *River Findhorn* — Clan Revan settled extensively in this river valley. |
|---|---|---|

**Septs**      MacCunn, MacSwan, MacSween, MacSwen, MacSwyle, Swan.

# Macrae

The name means 'Son of Grace' in Gaelic. The Macraes are said to have settled in Kintail in the fourteenth century, and they became Chamberlains of Kintail for several generations under the Mackenzies.

| PLACES of INTEREST | HIGHLAND SKYE AND LOCHALSH | *Eilean Donan,* 9 miles E of Kyle of Lochalsh, off A87. The castle was built in the thirteenth century, and held by the Macraes as Constables for the Mackenzies of Seaforth. Now restored, the Castle serves as a War Memorial for the Clan Macrae. Open Easter–September. |
|---|---|---|

**Septs**      Macara, MacCraw, Macra, Macrach, MacRaith, Macrath, Rae.

# MacThomas

Thomas, a Gaelic-speaking Highlander, known as Tomaidh Mor ('Great Tommy') was a descendant of the Clan Chattan Mackintoshes. He lived in the fifteenth century at a time when the Clan Chattan Federation had become large and unmanageable, so he took his kinsmen and followers across the Grampians from Badenoch to Glenshee. Iain Mor, 7th Chief, joined Montrose at Dundee in 1644. The Clan scattered after his death.

**PLACES of INTEREST**

**TAYSIDE**
**PERTH AND KINROSS**

*Finegand.* In about 1600, the 4th Chief, Robert McComie of the Thom was murdered. The chiefship passed to his brother, John McComie of Finegand, which is situated about three miles down Glenshee.

*Forter Castle* stands on B951 in Glenisla. It was purchased from Lord Airlie by Iain Mor in the seventeenth-century.

*Glen Prosen,* 10 miles NNE of Kirriemuir, Angus. McComie Mor's Putting Stone, McComie Mor's Wells and McComie Mor's Chair are physical attributes of the glen.

*Glenshee.* Early chiefs were settled at the Thom, on the east side of the Shee water, opposite the Spittal of Glenshee. The MacThomas Gathering Ground is located here.

**Septs**

Combe, Combie, McColm, McComas, McComb, McCombe, McCombie, McComie, McComish, MacOmie, MacOmish, Thom, Thomas, Thoms, Thomson.

# Maitland

A lowland family who rose to be Dukes of Lauderdale and played major roles in Scottish affairs for generations.

**PLACES of INTEREST**

**BORDERS**

ETTRICK AND LAUDERDALE — *Thirlestane Castle,* Lauder. Residence built by John Maitland of Thirlestane. Enlarged by the 1st Duke of Lauderdale. Privately owned.

**LOTHIAN**

EAST LOTHIAN — *Lennoxlove,* near Haddington on B6369. Formerly Lethington, home of the Maitlands from the fourteenth century. It incorporates a mediaeval tower. Bought in the eighteenth century by Lord Blantyre, and currently the seat of the Duke of Hamilton. To view telephone Haddington 3720.

EDINBURGH — *Queensberry House,* Canongate. Built in 1681 for Charles Maitland, later Earl of Lauderdale. Bought by the Duke of Queensberry. Now a hospital.

# Malcolm or MacCallum

The Malcolms come from a district of Lorn, in Argyllshire, and the name comes from a follower of Columba. Lands in Craignish and on the banks of Loch Avich were granted by Sir Duncan Campbell of Lochow to Reginald MacCallum of Corbarron in 1414. Dugald MacCallum of Poltalloch who inherited in 1779 adopted the name Malcolm permanently.

| PLACES of INTEREST | STRATHCLYDE | |
|---|---|---|
| | ARGYLL AND BUTE | *Craignish,* on B8002. Sixteenth-century keep. The MacCallums were appointed hereditary constables of the original castle in 1414. |
| | | *Duntrune Castle,* Kilmartin. Late sixteenth-century tower on the site of a thirteenth-century keep. Sold by the Campbells to Malcolms of Poltalloch in the eighteenth century. Privately owned. |
| | | *Poltalloch,* Loch Craignish. 10 miles N of Lochgilphead. Ancient seat of the clan. |

# Marjoriebanks

Walter, High Steward of Scotland, married Marjorie, only daughter of Robert Bruce and the Barony of Ratho was granted by the king to his daughter. These lands were denominated 'Terrae de Rath Marjorie banks', hence the name which was acquired by a family of the name of Johnstone.

| | |
|---|---|
| **PLACES of INTEREST** | **LOTHIAN** |
| | EAST LOTHIAN *Northfield House,* Prestonpans. Built 1611 for Joseph Marjoriebanks, an Edinburgh merchant. Privately owned. |
| | WEST LOTHIAN *Balbardie House,* Bathgate. Marjoriebanks house, undermined by subterranean tunnelling for coal and demolished in 1957, all save West Wing which remains amid modern houses. |

# Matheson (Mathieson)

The name means 'Son of the Bear'. The clan is an early offshoot of the Celtic earls of Ross and is said to have come from Lochalsh. There were two major branches — Lochalsh and Shinness, in Sutherland. From the former descend the Mathesons of Attadale and Ardross.

The Mathesons were involved in the sixteenth century with other clans who settled in Lochalsh, in particular the Macdonells of Glengarry and the Mackenzies of Kintail.

| **PLACES of INTEREST** | **HIGHLAND** | |
|---|---|---|
| | ROSS AND CROMARTY | *Attadale,* 5 miles NE of Stromeferry. Sold in 1825. Marriage between the vendor and a daughter of Matheson of Shinness reunited the houses of Matheson in Sutherland. |
| | SKYE AND LOCHALSH | *Eilean Donan,* 9 miles E of Kyle of Lochalsh, off A87. John *dubh* Matheson was the constable of this Mackenzie stronghold when it was besieged by Donald Gruamach of Sleat in 1539. He died in its defence. |

**Septs**    MacMahen, MacMath, Mathie.

# Maxwell

Sir John Maxwell, Chamberlain of Scotland in the thirteenth century seems to be the first recorded of the name. They held lands in Annandale and became Lords Maxwell and Earls of Nithsdale, and were for many years Wardens of the West March, and stewards of Annandale and Kirkcudbright. Prominent families are those of Pollok, Cardoness, Monreith and Farnham.

| **PLACES OF INTEREST** | **DUMFRIES AND GALLOWAY** | |
|---|---|---|
| | STEWARTRY | *Caerlaverock Castle,* 9 miles S of Dumfries. Thirteenth-century. Belonged to Lords Maxwell. Besieged by Edward I in 1300, and by Covenanters in 1638. Noted for its triangular design and tall fifteenth-century gatehouse. Open all year. *Merkland Cross,* Dumfries. Master of Maxwell murdered here 1484. *Threave Castle,* Castle Douglas, N of A75. Douglas Stronghold. Keepership invested in Maxwell, Earls of Nithsdale. Open all year. |
| | WIGTOWN | *Monreith Tower,* 5½ miles W of Whithorn, owned by Maxwells. Modern mansion. The writer Gavin Maxwell came from this family and there is a memorial to him on a hill overlooking Monreith Bay. *Myreton Castle,* W of Port William. Acquired by the Maxwells of Monreith from the McCullochs in 1685. Now in ruins. |
| | **STRATHCLYDE** | |
| | GLASGOW | *Pollok House.* Eighteenth-century, built by William Adam. Gifted to the City of Glasgow by the Stirling-Maxwells in 1967. Now houses part of the city's magnificent art collection. |

| INVERCLYDE | *Newark Castle,* Port Glasgow, off A8. Acquired by the Maxwells in 1402. Open all year. |
| RENFREW | *Haggs Castle,* 100 St Andrew's Drive, near Govan. Built by the Maxwells in 1585. Ruined, but partially restored and now incorporates a children's museum. |

# Menzies

A Norman name derived from Mayneris, near Rouen. The earliest definitive chief was Sir Robert de Meygners who became Chamberlain of Scotland in 1249. Records of the early history of the Menzies family were lost in a fire which destroyed the first castle at Weem in 1502, but it is probable that a branch of the family was granted lands in the Lothians in the twelfth century and eventually became established in the central Highlands. Extensive lands from Glendochart to Aberfeldy were granted to Sir Alexander Meygners, son of Sir Robert, for services to Robert Bruce. Bruce later bestowed on Sir Alexander the baronies of Glendochart and Durisdeer.

In later years, main Menzies territories settled around Weem, the Appin of Dull and Rannoch, and branches of the line became established in Pitfoddels (Aberdeenshire), Durisdeer (Nithsdale), Shian (Glenquaich), Culdares (Glenlyon), Rotmell (Dowally, Perthshire), Vogrie (Midlothian) and Culter (Lanark).

**PLACES of INTEREST**

**TAYSIDE**
PERTH AND KINROSS

*Castle Menzies,* 1½ miles NW of Aberfeldy. A Castle was erected at Weem (1 mile from Aberfeldy on B846) in 1488, but destroyed in a raid by Stewart of Garth in 1502. Castle Menzies which replaced it was erected in latter part of sixteenth century and is now owned by Menzies Clan Society. It is open April to September at weekends and at other times notified (admission charge). Nearby is the village of *Weem* and the Menzies Mausoleum; the Old Kirk of Weem, a pre-reformation church was the Parish church until 1840. It is notable for its Menzies Memorial, 1616.
*Comrie Castle* on the River Lyon was an early seat of the Menzies Clan. The ruin of a later keep on the site of the old can be seen (by bridge 4 miles west of Weem on B846).

# Moncreiffe

The name is taken from the lands of Moncreiffe which were gifted by Alexander II in 1248 to Sir Matthew Moncreiffe, who also held lands in Strathearn, Fife, and Atholl, probably by descent from Duncan I's brother Maldred (killed 1045). In 1586, William of that Ilk, 11th Chief, entered into a treaty with 'the haill Name of Murray' for their mutual defence.

| PLACES of INTEREST | TAYSIDE PERTH AND KINROSS | *Moncreiffe,* estate, 3 miles SE of Perth. On summit of hill there is a Fort which was once an important Pictish centre. Lands held by family since the thirteenth century. |
|---|---|---|

**Septs**  Moncreiff, Moncrieff, Moncrief.

# Montgomerie

Roger de Montgomerie, born about 1030, was joint Regent of Normandy when William the Conqueror invaded England in 1066. He was created Earl of Arundel. The first of the family in Scotland appears to be Robert de Mundegumrie, who died about 1177. He was granted Eaglesham, in Renfrewshire, and his descendant married the heiress of Sir Hugh de Eglinton, which brought the title of Earl of Eglinton in 1507.

| **PLACES of INTEREST** | **STRATHCLYDE** CUNNING-HAME | *Eaglesham,* 8½ miles S of Glasgow. Manor granted to Robert de Mundegumrie in twelfth century; retained in family for 700 years. *Eglinton Castle,* N of Irvine. Built in 1798: now ruined. Open to public. *Skelmorlie Castle,* Largs. Oldest part dates from 1502. Restored in 1852. Churchyard at Largs contains a monument to Sir Robert Montgomerie (d. 1651). |
| --- | --- | --- |

# Morrison

Said to be of Scandinavian origin, possibly from a natural son of a king of Norway cast ashore on the Isle of Lewis on a piece of driftwood. The Morrisons held the Hereditary Brieveship (judges of the island) of Lewis until 1613. They were deadly enemies of the Lewis MacAulays. For their services they were given lands around Ness, in Lewis. There were Morrisons in the counties of Perth, Stirling and Dunbarton, but they had no connection with the Lewis Morrisons.

| | |
|---|---|
| **PLACES of INTEREST** | **HIGHLAND** <br> WESTERN ISLES *Isle of Lewis* |
| **Septs** | Brieve, Gilmore, MacBrieve. |

# Mowat

Said to have settled in Scotland in the reign of King David I, they were of Norman origin. They moved to the North of Scotland, Orkney and Shetland.

| PLACES of INTEREST | GRAMPIAN | |
|---|---|---|
| | BANFF AND BUCHAN | *Hatton Castle,* Turriff. Thirteenth-century. Belonged to the Mowats until 1723. Privately owned. |
| | GORDON | *Woods of Brux,* near Bridge of Alford. Feud between Camerons and Mowats of Abergeldie to be settled by 12 horsemen of either side. The Mowats brought two men on each horse and massacred the Camerons. |

# Munro

A Ross-shire clan, ancient vassals of the Earls of Ross and originally from North Moray. The first chief was Hugh who lived in the twelfth century. William, 12th of Foulis, was knighted by James IV. The clan lands near Dingwall were called Ferindonald, after the supposed founder of the clan. The Munros supported the Government in the Jacobite risings.

| | | |
|---|---|---|
| **PLACES of INTEREST** | **HIGHLAND ROSS AND CROMARTY** | *Foulis Castle,* N of Dingwall. Eighteenth-century; seat of Chief. The Munro Museum is open to clan visitors. A condition of the clan's tenure was that a snowball be presented to the reigning monarch when passing. This could be obtained from nearby Ben Wyvis, never completely without snow. *Knock Fyrish,* Evanton, 6 miles NE of Dingwall. 'Indian Temple' on ridge (1483 feet) built by General Sir Hector Munro (1726-1805) of nearby Novar House as a means of easing local unemployment. |

**Septs**    Dingwall, Foulis, MacCulloch, MacLulich, Vass, Wass.

# Murray

Freskin de Moravia of Duffus, in Moray, acquired lands from David I his ancestor. He appears to have been chieftain of the Duffus branch of the Royal House of Moray. William de Moravia, his grandson, married the heiress to Bothwell and Drumsargard in Lanarkshire, and Smailholm in Berwickshire. From their son descend the Murrays of Tullibardine, forebears of the Dukes of Atholl. Other branches include Murrays of Abercairney, Earls of Mansfield and Lords Elibank.

Sir Andrew Moray of Bothwell fought with Wallace against Edward I, and Sir Andrew de Moravia was Regent of Scotland after the death of Robert Bruce.

---

**PLACES of INTEREST**

**GRAMPIAN**
MORAY

*Duffus Castle,* Lossiemouth, 4 miles NW of Elgin, off B9012. Fourteenth-century stronghold of the de Moravia family. Open to the public.

**TAYSIDE**
PERTH AND KINROSS

*Blair Castle,* Blair Atholl, on A9. Seat of Duke of Atholl. The castle dates back to 1269. Mary, Queen of Scots and Prince Charles Edward Stuart both stayed here, and it was besieged by General Lord George Murray while occupied by Hanoverian forces. The Duke of Atholl maintains the only legal private army in Scotland (the Atholl Highlanders). Open Easter Weekend, then May-October.
*Scone Palace,* Scone, 3 miles N of Perth, off A93. Built in 1803, and incorporating older buildings. Home of Murray Earls of Mansfield. Open April-October.

---

**Septs**   Dunsmore, Fleming, MacMurray, Moray, Piper, Pyper, Smail, Small, Smeal, Spalding.

# Napier

A name recorded as early as 1140, but the Heraldry of the Napiers of Merchiston shows a descent from the Lennox family.

Lord Napier, son of the inventor of Logarithms, married 1st Marquess of Montrose's sister.

| | | |
|---|---|---|
| **PLACES of INTEREST** | **LOTHIAN** EDINBURGH | *Lauriston Castle,* N of A90. Incorporates a sixteenth-century tower built by Sir Archibald Napier of Merchiston. *Merchiston Castle.* Fifteenth-century tower. Restored and used as the nucleus for Napier College, Edinburgh, in 1962. |

# Nicholson

The name arose in the Lowlands, but was found in Skye and Lewis, as a form of MacNicol. The Baronetcy was created 1629. A family is based on Fetlar in Shetland.

The Nicholsons of Lasswade — the Lowland line — descend from the Dean of Brechin in Angus.

# Ogilvy

Gillibride, second son of Ghillechriost, Earl of Angus, is the ancestor of this clan. He received the Barony of Ogilvy in the Parish of Glamis in about 1163. Sir Patrick de Ogilvy acquired the lands of Kettins in Angus, and his descendant, Sir Walter, obtained the Hereditary Sheriffship of Angus. Sir James became Lord Ogilvy of Airlie in 1491, and James 8th Lord, was created Earl of Airlie by Charles I in 1639. Clan lands included Glenisla, Glenprosen and Glenclova in Angus.

James, second son of the 3rd Earl of Findlater, and descended from the 8th Baron Ogilvy, who obtained the charter of the Lords of Airlie; became the first Earl of Seafield, in 1701.

| | | |
|---|---|---|
| **PLACES of INTEREST** | **LOTHIAN** | |
| | EAST LOTHIAN | *Winton Castle,* Pencaitland, on B6355. Seat of Ogilvy family since 1885. To view, telephone Pencaitland 340222. |
| | **TAYSIDE** | |
| | ANGUS | *Airlie Castle,* Kirriemuir. Ogilvy stronghold from 1430. Superseded by a mansion in 1763. Privately owned. *Cortachy Castle,* near Kirriemuir. Held by Airlies since the seventeenth century. Private home of the Earl of Airlie. *Farnell Castle,* Brechin. Built in 1512. Passed from Ogilvys to Carnegies 1623. Now an Old People's Home. *Forter Castle,* Glenisla. Sold to MacThomas clan. Now in ruins. *Glen Prosen.* Airlie Monument commemorates the 8th Earl (1856–1900) who fell in the South African war. *Inverquharity,* Glen Clova. For 400 years the seat of the Ogilvys. No admission. |

**Septs**  Airlie, Gilchrist, MacGilchrist, Milne.

# Oliphant

David de Olifard accompanied King David I from Winchester in 1141. They obtained lands of Gask and Aberdalgie from Robert Bruce, and the title of Lord Oliphant was conferred in 1458.

Oliphant is also a Sept name for Clan Sutherland.

---

**PLACES of INTEREST**

**FIFE**

NORTH EAST FIFE

*Kellie Castle,* Pittenweem, off A921. Mainly sixteenth- and seventeenth-century. Belonged to the Oliphants for 250 years until 1613 when it was acquired by the Erskines. Open Good Friday-September, daily except Fridays. National Trust for Scotland.

**TAYSIDE**

ANGUS

*Hatton Castle,* Newtyle. Built in 1575 by Laurence, 14th Lord Oliphant. Now a ruin.

PERTH AND KINROSS

*Ardblair Castle,* Blairgowrie, on A923. Lands granted by David II to Thomas Blair. Passed through marriage to Oliphants of Gask, in 1792. To view telephone Blairgowrie 2155.

# Ramsay

A family of ancient Anglo–Norman origin. The first recorded in Scotland was Simon de Ramsay, who was granted lands in Lothian by David I. They later became Lords Ramsay and Earls of Dalhousie.

The Ramsays of Bamff, Perthshire, are descended from Adam de Ramsay, a thirteenth-century baron.

| **PLACES of INTEREST** | **LOTHIAN** | |
|---|---|---|
| | MIDLOTHIAN | *Dalhousie Castle.* Owned by the Ramsays from the thirteenth century. Now a hotel. |
| | **TAYSIDE** | |
| | ANGUS | *Brechin Castle,* Brechin. Seat of Earl of Dalhousie. No admission. |
| | PERTH AND KINROSS | *Bamff House,* near Alyth. Lands held by Ramsays of Bamff from the early thirteenth century. The castle incorporates a sixteenth-century tower. |

# Rattray

A follower, but not a sept, of the Murrays of Atholl. The family descends from Adam de Rattrieff who was alive in the thirteenth century.

| PLACES of INTEREST | TAYSIDE | |
|---|---|---|
| | PERTH AND KINROSS | *Craighall,* Blairgowrie. Ancient seat of Rattrays. Privately owned. |

# Robertson
## Clan Donnachaidh

Duncan or *Donnachadh reamhair*, who led the clan for Bruce at Bannockburn, was descended from the Celtic earls of Atholl. From a later chief, Robert, in the reign of James I, comes the name Robertson. The barony of Struan was granted to Robert Duncanson by James II. The Robertsons rallied to the Stuart banner for Montrose and in the Jacobite risings. The residence was at Dunalastair, Kinloch Rannoch, and the clan was consistently a supporter of the House of Stuart.

| PLACES of INTEREST | TAYSIDE PERTH AND KINROSS | |
|---|---|---|
| | | *Clan Donnachaidh Museum,* Bruar Falls, Blair Atholl. Clan Headquarters. On A9. Open April–October. |
| | | *Struan,* 5 miles W of Blair Atholl. Ancient barony. |
| | | *Dunalastair,* to east of Loch Rannoch. Later residence was at Rannoch Barracks built by Hanoverian Government to control Clan Robertson *c.* 1751. |

**Septs**    Coller, Collier, Collyear, Donachie, Donochy, Duncan, Duncanson, Dunnachie, Inches, MacConnachie, MacDonachie, MacInroy, MacIver, MacIvor, MacLagan, MacRobbie, MacRobert, Ray, Reid, Stark.

# Rose

The family of Rose of Kilravock settled in Nairn in the reign of King David I. The Roses consistently supported the Government in 1688, 1715 and 1745.

**PLACES of INTEREST**

**HIGHLAND**
NAIRN

*Kilravock Castle,* Nairn. Built in 1460 by Hugh Rose of Kilravock. Added to in the seventeenth century. Prince Charles Edward Stuart was entertained here before Culloden while the Duke of Cumberland slept in a town house at Nairn. The Roses, however, were not Jacobites. No admission.

# Ross

Said to be of Norse origin, but probably descended from Gilleon na h-àirde, ancestor of Anrias, whose descendant, Fearcher MacinTagart, Earl of Ross, helped to crush a rebellion for the crown in 1215. For his services he was knighted, and recognised as Earl of Ross in 1234.

The earldom of Ross in the North was ancient and its possessors held enormous powers, judicial and otherwise. It was important to the southern-based Monarchs that the earldom was held by suitable representatives, and because of this, the title was awarded by successive monarchs to various holders. The Wolf of Badenoch married the widowed Countess of Ross, which enforced his position as Justiciar of the North.

Lands were acquired in Ayrshire and Renfrewshire by a family of Ross in the twelfth century.

| PLACES of INTEREST | HIGHLAND ROSS AND CROMARTY | *Balnagowan,* Easter Ross. Ancient chiefly house of Earls of Ross. No admission. |
|---|---|---|
| Septs | | Anderson, Andrew, Dingwall, Gillanders, MacAndrew, MacCulloch, MacLulich, MacTaggart, MacTear, Taggart, Vaas, Vass, Wass. |

# Russell

A name allied to the French Rosel. The Russells of Aden, in Aberdeenshire, descend from an English baron who accompanied Edward III at the siege of Berwick and decided to settle in Scotland.

# Scott

This is a Border clan descended from Uchtredus filius Scoti who lived in the twelfth century. His two sons were Richard, ancestor of the Scotts of Buccleuch, and Sir Michael, ancestor of the Scotts of Balweary.

The Barony of Buccleuch was created in 1606, and the Earldom in 1619. Francis, 2nd Earl, had two daughters, the second of whom married James, Duke of Monmouth. On their marriage in 1663 they were created Duke and Duchess of Buccleuch, each in their own right, and, although Monmouth was subsequently discredited and beheaded for rebellion, the Buccleuch title was passed to their children by the Duchess. A later marriage linked the Buccleuchs with the powerful Douglases, Dukes of Queensberry.

The Balweary line of Scott died out with the 7th Baronet of Ancrum, Sir William, known as 'The Wizard'. Hugh Scott, 11th of Harden, succeeded to the Barony of Polwarth and Sir Walter Scott's family are connected with this line.

| PLACES of INTEREST | | |
|---|---|---|
| | **BORDERS** | |
| | ETTRICK AND LAUDERDALE | *Abbotsford,* 2 miles W of Melrose, on the A7. The home of Sir Walter Scott, poet, patriot and novelist. Open to the public, March–October. |
| | | *Bowhill,* 4 miles SW of Selkirk on the A708 is the home of the Duke of Buccleuch and Queensberry. Open to the public, April–September, except Fridays. |
| | ROXBURGH | *Bellenden,* near the head of Ale Water, is the ancient gathering place of the Scotts. |
| | | *Branxholm Castle,* 3 miles SW of Hawick, is the ancient seat of the Scotts of Buccleuch. Privately owned. |
| | | *Harden,* Hawick, is the seat and private home of Lord Polwarth. |

## DUMFRIES AND GALLOWAY

STEWARTRY

*Drumlanrig Castle,* 3½ miles NW of Thornhill, off A76. Belongs to the Duke of Buccleuch. Built in 1679 over a former Douglas stronghold. Open to the Public.

## LOTHIAN

MIDLOTHIAN

*Dalkeith Palace.* Owned by the Buccleuch Estates, but houses Scottish Headquarters of ICL Ltd. Park open Easter–October.

# Scrimgeour

The name is recorded in the thirteenth century in connection with lands in Fife. Two documents issued in 1298 confirm lands on behalf of the Crown and Realm of Scotland by William Wallace and Robert Bruce. These confirm to Alexander Schyrmeschur, son of Colin, son of Carun, the perilous, but honourable privilege of carrying the king's banner in war, the office of constable of the castle of Dundee and certain lands in the Dundee neighbourhood. Later grants of land were near Inverkeithing, and through marriage to the heiress of Glassary.

| PLACES of INTEREST | | |
|---|---|---|
| **FIFE**<br>NORTH EAST FIFE | *Birkhill,* Cupar. Seat of the Earl of Dundee. No admission. |
| **TAYSIDE**<br>ANGUS | *Dudhope Castle,* Dundee. Built after Bannockburn to replace Dundee Castle. Seat of Scrymgeours, but acquired by Claverhouse in 1683. Privately owned. |

# Sempill

The Sempills come from Elliotstoun, in Renfrewshire; they are descendants of Robert de Semple (1280) and were hereditary Sheriffs of Renfrew. Sir John, 1st Lord Sempill died at Flodden. Maria Janet, Baroness Sempill was succeeded by her cousin, Sir William Forbes of Craigievar (descendant of Patrick Forbes of Corse, armour bearer to James III), who became 17th Lord Sempill in 1884.

| PLACES of INTEREST | GRAMPIAN | |
|---|---|---|
| | KINCARDINE AND DEESIDE | *Craigievar Castle,* Lumphanan, N of junction A974 and A980. Seventeenth-century tower built for William Forbes, an Aberdonian Merchant. Sempill Seat. National Trust for Scotland. Open May–September (except Fridays). |
| | STRATHCLYDE | |
| | RENFREW | *Peel Castle,* Lochwinnoch. Now in ruins. Situated in *Castle Semple Water Park,* Lochwinnoch (part of Clyde-Muirshiel Water Park). Semple Collegiate Church founded in 1504. Now in ruins. The Temple here is a folly built by Lady Sempill. |

# Seton

William the Lion gave a charter to Philip de Seton in 1169 of the Lands of Seton, Winton and Winchburgh. Further lands were granted to Sir Alexander Seton by Bruce in 1321. The Setons played a significant role in Scottish affairs and became Lords Seton, Earls of Dunfermline and Earls of Winton. They were passionate supporters of the Stuarts.

**PLACES of INTEREST**

**GRAMPIAN**
**BANFF AND BUCHAN GORDON**

*Seton Tower,* Fyvie Castle. Built by Alexander Seton, 1st Earl of Dunfermline.
*Pitmedden,* on B999, off A92. Seventeenth-century gardens, owned by Sir Alexander Seton. National Trust for Scotland. Open daily.

**LOTHIAN**
EAST LOTHIAN

*Seton Collegiate Church,* off A198. Fourteenth-century effigy of 3rd Lord Seton killed at Flodden. Open to public
*Seton House,* off A198. Rebuilt by Robert Adam in 1790, on the site of Seton Palace, home of 5th Lord Seton. Mary, Queen of Scots fled here after Rizzio's murder and after Darnley's murder. No admission.
*Winton Castle,* Pencaitland, on B6355. Said to have been built in 1480, by 1st Lord Seton. Destroyed by the English in 1544. Later castle was built in 1619 by the 8th Lord and 3rd Earl of Winton. The estate passed from the Setons in 1799. To view, telephone Pencaitland 340222.

EDINBURGH

*Gogar Castle,* Gogar, 5½ miles NW of Edinburgh. Given by King Robert I to Alexander Seton. Now has National Trust for Scotland's Gardening Advice Centre (Suntrap) in grounds.

WEST LOTHIAN

*Niddry Castle,* ½ mile S of Winchburgh. Ruined keep. Mary, Queen of Scots rode here after escape from Loch Leven. (No entrance to the keep; it can be viewed from the outside.)

# Shaw

### See Clan Chattan

The clan descends through Shaw, son of Gilchrist, grandson of 6th Chief of Clan Mackintosh. He was granted lands in Rothiemurchus in 1369. The Shaws of Tordarroch, descendants of Adam, 2nd son of Rothiemurchus, now hold the chiefship. They took protection from Clan Chattan.

| | | |
|---|---|---|
| **PLACES of INTEREST** | **HIGHLAND** | |
| | BADENOCH AND STRATHSPEY | *Castle of Loch-an-Eilean,* Loch-an-Eilean, Aviemore. B970. Ruins on island; Forest Visitor Centre on shore of loch. |
| | | *Dunlichty Parish Church,* 6 miles from Daviot is where Shaw chiefs are buried. Now in ruins. |
| | **STRATHCLYDE** | |
| | INVERCLYDE | *Greenock* was a burgh of Barony held by the Shaws until 1741. |

**Septs**   Adamson, Ayson (NZ), Esson, MacAy, MacHay, Scaith, Seith, Seth, Shaith, Shay, Sheach, Sheath, Shiach.

# Sinclair

Sir William Saint Clair, son of Robert de Saint Clair in Normandy, seemingly founded this clan. His son, Sir Henry de Sancto Claro, supported Robert Bruce and signed the letter to the Pope in 1320 asserting Scotland's independence.

Sinclair of Roslin, a grandson, married a co-heiress of Malise, Earl of Strathearn, Caithness and Orkney. His eldest son obtained from King Hakon VI of Norway, the right to the Earldom of Orkney and received the Earldom of Caithness in 1455. In 1470, the Earldom of Orkney was resigned to the Scottish crown in exchange for Ravenscraig Castle.

| | | |
|---|---|---|
| **PLACES of INTEREST** | **HIGHLAND** CAITHNESS | *Castle of Mey,* 7 miles W of John o' Groats, on A836. Built in 1568 by George, 5th Earl of Caithness. Now the residence of Queen Elizabeth the Queen Mother (open 3 days a year in aid of charity). |

*Castle of Mey,* 7 miles W of John o' Groats, on A836. Built in 1568 by George, 5th Earl of Caithness. Now the residence of Queen Elizabeth the Queen Mother (open 3 days a year in aid of charity).

*Keiss Castle,* Keiss. Remains of a small sixteenth-century tower. The nineteenth-century castle nearby was the home of Sir William Sinclair, founder and pastor of the first Baptist Church in Scotland.

*Noss Head,* Wick. Castles Sinclair (fifteenth-century) and Girnigoe (seventeenth-century). Residences of Earls of Caithness. The estates were invaded by the Campbell of Glenorchy in 1679. Both castles were destroyed.

*Thurso Castle,* Thurso. Sir John Sinclair (1754-1835), well known agricultural improver lived here. No admission.

**LOTHIAN** MIDLOTHIAN

*Roslin,* off A701. Ruins of fourteenth-century castle. Fifteenth-century chapel (with carved 'Prentice Pillar').

**Septs**      Caird, Clouston, Clyne, Gallie, Linklater, Mason.

# Skene

It is said that the founder of this clan was offered by Malcolm Canmore as much land as was covered by a hawk's flight, and thus was formed the Barony of Skene in Aberdeenshire. The Skenes of Skene became extinct in 1827.

| PLACES of INTEREST | GRAMPIAN | |
|---|---|---|
| | ABERDEEN | *Skene's House,* Aberdeen. Home of Sir George Skene (1619–1707), Provost. Acquired by the city and now a museum. |
| | GORDON | *Skene Castle,* Skene. Part–eighteenth-century. Privately owned. |

**Septs**     Cariston, Dis, Dyce, Hallyard, Norrie.

# Stewart

Galloway

Appin

The Royal House of Stewart, whose traditional descent was of old derived from Banquo, Thane of Lochaber, has been historically traced to Alan, Seneschal of Dol, a Celtic noble. His nephew became Sheriff of Shropshire in England, and his third son, Walter Fitz Alan, became High Steward of Scotland in the reign of David I. He founded Paisley Abbey. The office of High Steward was confirmed as an Hereditary Office by Malcolm IV. Walter's grandson, Walter, was the first to adopt the title of 'Steward' as a surname. Walter, 6th High Steward, married Marjory, daughter of King Robert Bruce.

The origins of the Stewarts in Scotland are essentially Lowland. They were the staunchest upholders of national liberty, and one should not forget that all that Bruce won was lost in the minority of his son, Scotland being again over-run by English. The prime instrument of recovery and final establishment of his country's freedom was gained by Bruce's grandson, Robert Stewart, 7th Hereditary High Steward of Scotland, later Robert II, first of the Royal House of Stewart.

The Stewarts were a remarkably prolific race, and had many offspring, legitimate and otherwise. Sir John of Bonkyl (d. 1298) had seven sons — among them Alexander, Earl of Angus, Alan, Earl of Lennox, Walter, progenitor of the Earls of Galloway, and James, progenitor of the Earls of Buchan and Traquair as well as the Lords of Lorne and Innermeath. (Since the demise of the Lennoxes, Earl of Galloway has been regarded as the senior representative of the ancient line of High Stewards of Scotland.) One can appreciate how the Stewarts then multiplied and spread throughout Scotland. In 1463, Sir John Stewart of Lorne was murdered, and his son Dugald sought to recover the Lordship from his uncle. By compromise, he received the lands from Appin. Allan, 3rd of Appin, established the Appin clan by dividing the lands between his five sons.

The Stewarts of Atholl descend from Sir John Stewart of Balveny, half-brother of James II. Dorothea, daughter of the 5th Earl, was wife of the 2nd Earl of Tullibardine, and so the Earldom passed into the Murray clan.

The Stuarts of Bute are descended from a natural son of King Robert II. He was known as the 'Black Stewart' to distinguish him from his brother, John of Dundonald, nicknamed, the 'Red Stewart'.

Many of the Stewart kings came to a violent end. James I was murdered at Perth in 1437; James II was killed by a bursting cannon at the siege of Roxburgh in 1460; James III died as he fled from the battlefield of Sauchieburn in 1488; James IV married Margaret Tudor, daughter of Henry VII of England, and was killed at Flodden in 1513 in battle against his brother-in-law, King Henry VIII; James V married Mary of Guise and died in 1542, three weeks after the rout at Solway Moss.

Mary, James V's only daughter, was married to Dauphin Francis of France in 1558. He became King of France in 1559 and died in 1560. When Mary returned to her own realm, it was to a turbulent and divided land. Her policies were successful and popular until her marriage to Henry, Lord Darnley, eldest son of the Earl of Lennox, and through Margaret Douglas, Countess of Lennox, a great-grandson of Henry VII of England. This marriage ensured that their son, James, became heir to the thrones of both kingdoms.

Darnley's murder in 1567 and Mary's marriage to the Earl of Bothwell led to her downfall and flight to England. She was executed in 1587 for alleged plotting against Queen Elizabeth I of England.

Mary's son James VI was an astute but devious ruler. Not for nothing was he known as 'The Wisest Fool'. In 1603 he became King of England, and moved his court to London. He died in 1625.

Charles I's policy of challenging Parliament and asserting his 'divine right' led to his execution at Whitehall in 1649, and a period of rule by the 'Commonwealth'. The Scots agreed to bring Charles II from exile in Holland if he signed the Covenants. He was crowned at Scone in 1651, returned to exile, and was restored to the English throne in 1660, after Cromwell's death. He died in 1685 and his brother became James VII and II. His Catholic faith was unacceptable to many, and when there was a revolution in support of his daughter Mary and her husband, William of Orange, devout Protestants, James was forced to flee overseas.

William and Mary had no heir, and Mary's sister, Queen Anne, also died without heir. In 1673, James VII and II married Mary of Modena, a Catholic princess. Their son, James Francis, became known as the 'Old Pretender'. Catholicism was unacceptable to the Whig government; they therefore approached a great-grandson of James VI and

I, the Protestant George of Hanover, who became King of England and Scotland in 1714.

In 1715, the Old Pretender landed at Peterhead to join the Earl of Mar in an uprising against the Hanoverians; but he departed soon after, and spent the rest of his life in Rome, where he died in 1766. His elder son, Prince Charles Edward, 'Bonnie Prince Charlie', is the best known of the Stuarts, the 'kings across the water'. The uprising he led in 1745 was crushed at Culloden. He died in Rome in 1788, and was succeeded as *de jure* king by his brother, styled Henry IX, a Cardinal of the Church of Rome, who died in 1807. The Jacobite claim to the Scottish throne has now passed to the Duke of Bavaria.

| | | |
|---|---|---|
| **PLACES of INTEREST** | **The Royal Stewarts** | |
| | **HIGHLAND** | |
| | INVERNESS | *Culloden Moor,* scene of Prince Charles Edward Stuart's final defeat 16 April 1746. The National Trust for Scotland has an information centre and museum here. |
| | LOCHABER | *Glenfinnan.* Prince Charles Edward's standard was first raised here on 19 August 1745.<br>*Loch nan Uamh,* off A830, SE of Arisaig. Scene of Prince Charles Edward Stuart's landing and departure. There is a commemorative stone cairn. |
| | **LOTHIAN** | |
| | EDINBURGH | *Holyrood Palace* has many associations with Stewart monarchs, particularly Mary Queen of Scots and Prince Charles Edward Stuart.<br>*Edinburgh Castle* was the birthplace of King James VI in 1566. It houses 'The Honours of Scotland'. |

## LOTHIAN

WEST LOTHIAN | *Linlithgow Palace* was the birthplace of Mary, Queen of Scots in 1542.

STIRLING | *Stirling Castle* and *Church of the Holy Rude*. Mary, Queen of Scots was crowned at Stirling in 1543; James VI was baptised here in 1566 and crowned here in 1567.

## TAYSIDE

PERTH AND KINROSS | *Loch Leven Castle*, on Loch Leven was where Mary, Queen of Scots was held prisoner from 1567–68.
*Doune Castle*, overlooking River Teith. Off A84. Built towards end of fourteenth century by Robert Stewart, Regent of Scotland and Duke of Albany in the reign of Robert III. Restored ruin, owned by Earl of Moray. Open to public April–Oct. (excl. Thurs.), June–Aug. (all week).

Doune Castle

**FIFE**

NORTH EAST
FIFE

*Falkland Palace.* A912. Hunting Lodge of the Stewart Kings. James V died here after his defeat at Solway Moss in 1542. (National Trust for Scotland.) Open April–Oct.

**Stewarts of Appin**
**BORDERS**

TWEEDDALE

*Traquair House,* Innerleithen. B709 off A72. Reputed to be oldest inhabited house in Scotland. Bear gates 'never to be re-opened until a Stewart returns to the throne'. Sir John Stuart, 1st Earl of Traquair was Lord High Treasurer of Scotland in the reign of Charles I. Open May–Oct.

**DUMFRIES AND**
**GALLOWAY**

WIGTOWN

*Galloway House,* Garlieston. Seat of the Earls of Galloway. House is privately owned, but the gardens are open to the public.

**HIGHLAND**

BADENOCH
AND
STRATHSPEY

*Lochindorb,* or *Loch of the Trout,* unclassified road off A939, built by the Comyns, was famous as stronghold of the 'Wolf of Badenoch' (1342–1406),

Robert II's notorious son. The Island with its ruined castle can be seen from the road.

## HIGHLAND

| | |
|---|---|
| LOCHABER | *Ballachulish*. Association with the Appin murder 1752. Site of execution of James Stewart in Acharn for 'art and part' in the murder of Colin Campbell of Glenure, the King's factor on the forfeited estate of Ardsheal. |
| MORAY | *Elgin*. The Cathedral was burnt by Wolf of Badenoch in 1389. |

## STRATHCLYDE

| | |
|---|---|
| ARGYLL AND BUTE | *Ardsheal House* was home of the Stewarts of Appin, now a hotel. *Castle Stalker*. Offshore from A828. Fifteenth century Stewart of Appin stronghold and hunting seat. It is privately owned and recently renovated. *Mount Stuart* is seat of the Marquess of Bute. *Rothesay Castle* was used by Robert II and III, James IV and V. |

## TAYSIDE

| | |
|---|---|
| PERTH AND KINROSS | *Dunkeld*. Wolf of Badenoch's tomb and effigy is in Cathedral. |

# Sutherland

"South Land", i.e. south of Caithness and Orkney, is the origin of this name. The inhabitants of Sutherland are considered to descend from the Celts who retreated before the Norse invaders. The chiefs originate with Freskin, progenitor of the Murrays. His youngest son Hugh Freskin received the lands from King William the Lion in 1197. They became Earls and Dukes of Sutherland.

| PLACES of INTEREST | HIGHLAND | |
|---|---|---|
| | ROSS AND CROMARTY | *Carbisdale*, N of Ardgay. Built by Duchess of Sutherland in nineteenth century. Now a Youth Hostel. |
| | SUTHERLAND | *Ben Braggie*, Golspie. Statue of 1st Duke of Sutherland who died 1833 looks over town. He built Golspie and was blamed for Clearance evictions. |
| | | *Dornoch Cathedral*, Dornoch. Major restoration sponsored by the Duchess of Sutherland between 1835 and 1837. Sixteen earls of Sutherland lie in Cathedral. |
| | | *Dunrobin*, Golspie, off A9. Said to be ancient, but virtually all present building is Victorian. Seat of Countess of Sutherland. Open May–September. |
| | | *Helmsdale Castle*, Helmsdale. 1488. Scene of murder of 11th Earl in 1567. |

**Septs**     Cheyne, Federeth, Gray, Keith, Mowat, Oliphant.

# Turnbull

For saving the life of King Robert Bruce when he was attacked by a wounded bull, one William of Rule was awarded lands and was thereafter known as Turn-e-bull.

The Rule Water territory of the Turnbulls was a baronial possession of the house of Douglas. By 1510, the Turnbulls had become so scornful of the authority of King James IV that he decided to make an example of them and 200 members of the family appeared before him wearing linen sheets, swords in hands and halters around their necks. Some were hanged and some were imprisoned.

The unsettled state of the Borders, however, continued, causing King James VI to order his wardens to use "hostile feud in hostile manner against all malefactors". Many families left at this time. The chief branches of Bedrule and Minto fell into financial difficulties, and scattered.

**PLACES of INTEREST**

**BORDERS**

ROXBURGH

*Barnshills Castle,* N side of River Teviot, near base of Minto Crags. Ivy covered ruins. Built sixteenth century.

*Bedrule Castle,* Rule Valley. Ruins two hundred yards from Bedrule Church. Destroyed by English 1545.

*Fulton Tower,* on right bank of the Rule Water.

*Minto Estate* on River Teviot. Held by Turnbulls before passing through various owners to Elliots in seventeenth century.

*Philiphaugh Estates.* These lands in Ettrick Forest held for 300 years. Murrays acquired part of lands through marriage, and then entirely after last of Turnbull name died in 1572.

# Urquhart

Surname derives from lands of Urquhart of Cromarty
Firth. William Urquhart, Sheriff of Cromartie, married a
daughter of the Earl of Ross in fourteenth century.

| **PLACES of INTEREST** | | |
|---|---|---|
| | **GRAMPIAN** | |
| | BANFF AND BUCHAN | *Craigston Castle,* off B9105, 10 miles SE of Banff. Seat of Urquhart family since 1604-07. To view: telephone King Edward 228. |
| | **HIGHLAND** | |
| | ROSS AND CROMARTY | *Castle Craig,* Udale Bay on Cromarty Firth. Ancestral fortress. Now ruin. |

# Wallace

The name Wallace means 'Strathclyde Briton' and is therefore a 'native' name. The name was predominant in the thirteenth century in Ayrshire and Renfrewshire. Richard Wallace (or Wallensis) of Richardston or Riccarton, who lived in the twelfth century, is the first noted of the name. Richard was in the service of Walter Fitzalan, first Steward of Scotland. His grandson, Adam, had two sons, Adam, 4th Earl of Riccarton in Ayrshire, and Malcolm, who received the lands of Elderslie and Auchinbothie, in Renfrewshire, and this latter was the father of Scotland's hero, Sir William Wallace (1274–1305) who led the revolt against English rule before his violent demise and the advent on the battlefield of Robert Bruce.

The Wallaces of Craigie, Ayrshire, are also descended from those of Riccarton.

| | | |
|---|---|---|
| **PLACES of INTEREST** | **BORDERS** ETTRICK AND LAUDERDALE | *Dryburgh Abbey.* In the trees to the north of the Abbey stands a huge statue of Wallace erected in 1814. *Selkirk, St Mary's Church.* Believed to be where Sir William Wallace was elected Guardian of Scotland. |
| | **CENTRAL** STIRLING | *Wallace Memorial* built 1896 stands on top of Abbey Craig. Off A997. |
| | **DUMFRIES AND GALLOWAY** NITHSDALE | *Wallace's House.* Ruins on the Garvald Water in the south of the forest supposedly the tower garrisoned by Sir William in 1297. |
| | **STRATHCLYDE** KYLE AND CARRICK RENFREW | *Ayr, Wallace Tower,* High Street. Built 1828. *Elderslie,* 9 miles west of Glasgow. Memorial on A737. |

GLASGOW

William Wallace was captured at *Robroyston* and handed over to the English who took him to London for trial and execution.

LANARK

*Lanark:* statue of Wallace by sculptor Robert Forrest, presented to the town in 1882. It commemorates the tradition of the murder of Wallace's wife, Marian Bradfute, who came from Lanark.

# Some useful addresses

**HIGHLAND**
INVERNESS

*An Comunn Gaidhealach,* Abertarff House, Church Street, Inverness.
*The Highlands and Islands Development Board,* Bridge House, Bank Street, Inverness.

**LOTHIAN**
EDINBURGH

*The Lyon Office,* New Register House, Edinburgh, 1.
*The National Museum of Antiquities,* 1 Queen Street, Edinburgh.
*Scots Ancestry Research Society,* 3 Albany Street, Edinburgh EH1 3PY.
*The National Trust for Scotland,* 5 Charlotte Square, Edinburgh, 2.
*The Scottish Experience,* St Thomas' Church, Rutland Place, Edinburgh. Large scale model of Scotland; audio visual displays.
*The Scottish Tourist Board,* Ravelston Terrace, Edinburgh, 4.
*Scotworld Club,* The Caledonian Club, 33 Abercromby Place, Edinburgh. Membership organisation for people of Scottish descent living overseas.

**TAYSIDE**
PERTH AND
KINROSS

*The Museum of Scottish Tartans,* Drummond Street, Comrie. Run by the Scottish Tartans Society, this houses the largest collection in existence of material relating to tartans and Highland dress. Open all year.

# Index of places mentioned in the text